PARIS

1. 22, rue Barbet de Jouy
2. Musée Rodin
3. Shops at rue de Bourgogne
4. M. Caro, the barber
5. Bon Marché department store
6. Pont Alexandre III
7. Jardins des Tuilleries
8. Parc Monceau, Ecole Bilinque
9. Place d'Etoile
10. La Tour Eiffel
11. Euromarché

N

An American Family In Paris

Letters from the 7th Arrondissement

An American Family In Paris

Letters from the 7th Arrondissement

Sally Fallon Morell

Cover and Illustrations by Richard Morris

Published by:

NewTrends Publishing, Inc.

Brandywine, Maryland 20613

Order Line (877) 707-1776
www.newtrendspublishing.com
customerservice@newtrendspublishing.com

Available to the trade through
National Book Network 800-462-6420

First printing: 20,000

ISBN
0-9823383-5-X, 978-0-9823383-5-3
PRINTED IN THE UNITED STATES OF AMERICA

Preface

Looking back – it's thirty years since we lived in Paris – I realize how so much came together to create the sparkling jewel that was our sojourn in the City of Light. For one thing, we had friends there – John's business acquaintances and office workers, and also friends of my parents (who were frequent travelers to France). These friends had introduced me to their daughters of my age. The French can be standoffish, but once they become your friends, they shower you with delightful conversation and charm.

John's work running the Paris office for a company that sold equipment to airline manufacturers was another plus. It was interesting work and led to many interesting friendships.

Then there was the economic situation: it was only the strong dollar that allowed us to rent the beautiful apartment in the 7th arrondissement. At one point during our stay, every dollar was worth ten francs, which meant that we paid less for the apartment than we got for our rented house at home, and a bottle of good wine could be had for under five dollars.

Our children were at a perfect age to learn French, with their flexible young minds, and as parents we could observe French customs about children from birth to pre-adolescence. We were young and therefore energetic – bringing up children, especially four childen, in Paris is not easy.

During those years, I never imagined that I would later become a writer of cookbooks or, for that matter, that anyone would need to come to the defense of animal fats and cholesterol. Who could have predicted the assault on foods that make life worth living: pâté and butter, eggs and cream? We lived just one block from La Varenne, the famous cooking school, but I never had time to take their course.

I did, however, take classes put on by the American Women in Paris. The instructor was Irish, so naturally we got the real basics of French cooking, including stocks of every type: chicken, beef, duck, fish and shrimp. We learned to make *magret de canard* and *confit*, we learned *bechamel* and *soufflé à l'orange*. Most importantly, we mastered that quintessence of French cuisine: reduction sauces. I doubt I would have come away from a year's course at La Varenne with such a wide array of skills.

Another thing: we did not have the Internet in those days. Computers were new; we had one there but it was a novelty we used mostly for games. Had we access to the Internet, would we have spent so much time on the streets and in the parks?

Thirty years have passed: the children are scattered to the four winds, and John has moved on to those Elysian Fields. Likewise, most of our friends have died or lost touch. Madame Dupuy, the quintessential French *arriviste*, is gone. But Florence has become famous, a spokeswomen for women's rights in France. Helge has achieved fame as well, as a concert pianist with many recordings.

Thank goodness I wrote everything down, or many of the details would have disappeared into the dark hole of forgetfulness. Only recently I fished these letters from the file cabinet; they were saved onto a floppy disk that no longer fits into modern computers.

On a recent trip to Paris, after a long absence, I visited the old neighborhood. Little has changed. The fish market on rue de Bourgogne has disappeared, but most of the other shops are there, even M. Caro's place still functions as a hair salon. Deyrolle, the taxidermist, is still in business and now has a website and Facebook page. The old convent has undergone conversion to apartments, but the garden is still a public place where children can walk on the grass. Students at L'Ecole Bilingue next to Parc Monceau still learn French and English.

The Bon Marché department store, however, has been spruced up beyond recognition and now sells merchandise at prices that make you gasp. They have moved the lingerie section away from the entrance, and the polyester dress department has disappeared.

The biggest change I encountered: very few restaurants make real stock or reduction sauces anymore.

Still, the French behave as they always have. In a café, I sat next to a couple enjoying lunch together. He began his meal with a plate of snails; his slim companion spooned out the contents of an enormous marrow bone. Then they had steak cooked rare and fries. They finished with dessert and coffee. They consumed a whole bottle of red wine. I doubt they were married because they talked to each other the whole time.

Sally Fallon Morell
August, 2015

1983

e always swore we would never send a letter with the Christmas card, one of those cheerful, numbing accounts of the children, the pets, the job and recovery from skiing injuries; but that was before we established a household on French soil a year ago with John's transfer to Paris.

It was just after last Christmas when I left Los Angeles on Air France flight 004, non-stop to Paris, along with twenty assorted suitcases, duffle bags and boxes. These contained the worldly goods the children and ourselves had needed to survive a six-week stay at the Ambassador Hotel. (One of those duffle bags contained roller skates and lunch boxes.) Two rooms there – smelling of nylon carpet and Bunsen burners – had served as home during the several weeks it took our furniture to cross the Atlantic. I had ahead of me a quiet plane ride with a good book and a week to take care of unpacking and stocking up before John would arrive with the children: Sarah, age nine, Nicholas, age five and James, age two. We were expecting the arrival of child number four in March.

In a less advanced stage of pregnancy I had traveled to Paris with John in October to look at apartments and schools. It was not our first trip to Paris; both of us had lived there in happy penury as students and had visited her in more prosperous circumstances as tourists and business travelers. As we both spoke passable French and had friends in France, we welcomed the assignment and were eager to move. One of those friends used her influence to help us enroll Sarah and Nicholas mid-year in *Ecole Bilingue*, a French-run bilingual school near Parc Monceau.

We were determined to make the immersion of the children as total as possible – French schools, French friends, and an apartment in the city of Paris, rather than a house in the suburbs with garden, driveway and nearby shopping malls.

In our search for apartments John and I saw a side of Paris we hadn't known as tourists and visitors: the family-sized apartment, built to satisfy the Parisian's dual requirements of privacy and display.

The first we saw was typical of many – living and dining rooms of splendid proportions and well lit, the bedrooms smaller and darkened with heavy draperies. The kitchen was a dirty and depressing room at the end of a long hall, a long walk from the dining room. Along this hall were several other little rooms, one a laundry room where two housekeepers worked lazily through a pile of washing and ironing.

The two girls presumably carried food down the long corridor from the kitchen to the dining room at mealtimes. For the Frenchman this arrangement performs the practical function of preventing eaves-dropping by the servants, but it did not seem a very practical arrangement for an American family with young children.

In the evening we visited a similar apartment and found again two girls, this time in starched uniforms, peeling radishes. The kitchen in which they worked was filthy and dark, the size of a closet, but the living room was grandly draped, like the inside of a circus tent, with bands of fabric running to the center of the ceiling. There sat Monsieur and Madame and their children waiting for those radishes and the rest of dinner.

Massive wardrobes, padding and draperies in the bedrooms created an atmosphere of claustrophobic, stifling intimacy. We wanted light and space and closets. The real estate agent raised our spirits with the promise of something better in the morning. "An apartment completely redone," he explained, "and full of light." It had four bedrooms and was close to the children's school. It sounded perfect.

The front door of this perfect apartment opened onto a small vestibule leading to another room, clean and white. It was full of light, lacking curtains. At the end of this bright room a door opened onto the apartment's first – and only – closet, which contained built-in drawers, a hot plate on a counter and another door leading to a long corridor. This hall had five doors in succession, four of which opened onto small rooms, like cubicles (two with windows and two without); the fifth door for the bathroom. The agent had to explain to us – sheepishly – that the vestibule was the living room, the one room of decent size for dining, and the closet – "Of course that is the kitchen, Madame," and the four small rooms, the four bedrooms.

The apartment had indeed suffered a renovation; it was split off from a larger apartment and two rooms of moderate size divided to produce a four-bedroom apartment. After that we were careful to explain that we had three children, and one on the way, that as Americans we indulged in certain strange habits, like eating breakfast, and that our one fundamental requirement was what American real estate agents refer to as ESIK – eating space in kitchen. That, Madame, Monsieur, would be more difficult.

Next we were shown an enormous apartment in the 8th arrondissement. It had plenty of rooms, all large, and ceilings of gesso work. Plaster cupids peered down from the cornices, their curly heads and every surface bearing the patina of ancient dirt. A sink in the corner distinguished the bedrooms from the living rooms or *salons*, these conveniences no doubt hidden by screens when the apartment was in its furnished state. One water closet served the entire apartment of seven bedrooms, and those who wished a bath could wash in a small tin tub on feet, standing in the largest of the bedrooms.

The kitchen did indeed have ESIK and nothing else. A few wires and clamped off pipes peaked through holes in the walls and you could see the outlines of vanished cupboards. But the kitchen was empty, stripped bare.

At this point we learned one fundamental fact about apartments in Paris – what you rent is the four walls, the floors and ceilings, and anything that cannot be removed from said surfaces without excessive damage to same. If the previous tenant has made any improvements, if he has installed a bathroom or kitchen cabinets – the owner of the building never does this – you must negotiate with the tenant to pay him for the additions he has made. If you fail to come to an agreement over this *reprise*, he has the right to remove, and indeed surely will, every light fixture, shelf, hook and toilet paper holder in the apartment. We gulped, and asked to see some apartments that were "improved."

When we stepped up to improved apartments, we had a great deal more to see but no fewer problems. One beautiful apartment in the 16th had legal encumbrances requiring a year to untangle. Another was decorated like a Grecian temple, with false columns and working fountains for the enjoyment of the children.

A third, also in the 16th, had a garden, but the improvements, offered to us at an inflated price, included extensive wall coverings of padded grey velvet, difficult to touch up after stabbings with crayons or toys. But seeing the garden led us to ask if there were not, just possibly, any houses to rent in Paris.

In France a freestanding city house is called a *hôtel particulier* and there were, in fact, two *hôtels* then available. The Embassy of Luxembourg had just relinquished its lease. We could have this mansion for a mere million dollars a year. The other was a three-story house with a large garden in the 15th arrondissement.

The agents assured us that we wouldn't want it, and they were right. The first floor had no windows, the other floors lacked the simplest amenities. The garden, choked with weeds and shaded by surrounding buildings, seemed particularly dreary in the rain. The house had one improvement: a wrought iron entrance gate in the form of a spider web, complete with spider in the upper corner. The owner, a veiny-cheeked man wearing a beret, took his time to show us every cupboard and corner but failed to convince us that this was the place for us.

Just as the agents had run through their lists of available apartments, a new one came on the market, an apartment occupying two floors in the 7th. The tenant, a German woman, had tax problems (having never paid any) and had to leave France immediately.

The money saved in taxes had paid for masterfully tasteless decoration of her apartment; it was obvious she had fallen into the clutches of some ungovernable decorator bent on obliterating any traces of the old France. He had installed modern appurtenances and Lurex draperies throughout; his favorite paint color was black. The dining room, painted in funereal tones, served as a billiard room (and doubled as a casino, we later learned) while one bedroom had brown spots of various sizes painted on the wall, to resemble cowhide. Fortunately her decorator lacked the nerve to cover over the eighteenth century oak paneling in the living room.

The apartment was a *duplex*; that is, an apartment with two floors (occupying the second and third floors in the front of the building), with two living rooms or *salons*, dining room and kitchen on the first floor and bedrooms on the second. Along with six marble fireplaces (none working), the apartment had two modern bathrooms, three large and two small bedrooms, several closets, and a remodeled kitchen lacking any trace of the old France. It contained – in addition to stove, ovens, dishwasher, open rotisserie and built-in deep fat fryer – a built-in table for the feeding of young children.

The loss in revenues to the nation of France was to be our gain. Negotiations began immediately, Madame-the-tax-evader only too happy to take a loss on the kitchen installation for payment in dollars.

There followed a series of four meetings, each several hours long, and involving a lawyer each for the owner, the tenant, the real estate agents and ourselves. Four times we joined these lawyers as they closeted themselves in an unventilated room; four times we watched the ashtrays fill up as they discussed minor points of the contract.

Fortunately, I returned to Los Angeles before the discussions ended, leaving John to formally obtain our apartment at 22, rue Barbet de Jouy and, incidentally, to begin work in Paris. (We have taken perverse delight in pointing out to French friends the ease with which we rented our Los Angeles house after our move to Paris – one form contract and two long-distance phone calls settled everything.)

It was to 22, rue Barbet de Jouy that a co-worker of John's brought me on the night of my arrival in Paris. The apartment, empty and echo-y, welcomed me nevertheless with the promise of a new home and a new lifestyle, more stylish, more stylized than the casual ways of California. The furniture would arrive in several days. Meanwhile I had a list of items to accomplish on my own – not as a tourist this time, but as a member of a more coveted class and the envy of Francophiles, a resident of the city of Paris.

What most impresses the native Californian, finding herself displaced to Paris in midwinter? It is the sky – usually grey, but even when cloudless a pale and icy color of blue. I did miss the acetate blue sky and bright sunlight of California those first few weeks. But Paris is an elegant lady and looks poorly in synthetics. The displaced Californian soon learns to appreciate the attenuated light of the Paris sky as the most appropriate background for her architectural splendors.

My first sortie, that first grey day in Paris, was to the bank to open an account. In France this is not the fifteen-minute exercise that it is in America. You must fill out numerous forms, supply references and submit to credit checks. I met with a Madame Rehaume who explained French banking regulations – woefully complicated – using a lot of words I had never encountered in French classes; and she didn't deign to speak slowly for me, an unimportant client. But I did understand that it would take some time and several more visits to the bank before I could transfer money, write a check and withdraw cash.

When God apportioned out talents among his peoples he gave liberally of artistic and intellectual skills to the French, but shorted them in patience, so that sooner or later tourist and expatriate alike must experience the Frenchman in anger. This happened to me the day I took the car out of the garage – I was headed for Darty, an appliance store under the Madeleine, to buy an iron, a toaster and a vacuum cleaner.

The ex-tenant of our apartment, now safely outside the borders of France, had rented a parking spot in an underground garage across the street. We had assumed her lease, and John had left our newly acquired car in the space she told us was hers before he returned to California for Christmas. But she had not correctly remembered the number of the space (no doubt distracted by her tax woes) so the car had sat in another person's – in another Frenchman's – parking spot for several weeks.

When I emerged from the garage, already apprehensive about my first drive in Paris, the *gardien* accosted me, shouting and raving about our mistaken appropriation, as no doubt the lessee of the usurped space had shouted at him. With my hesitant French, I was no match for him. Only when I got out of the car and he realized he was heaping invective on a woman in advanced pregnancy, did he calm down. The car, he explained, was in a spot inaccessible to a tow truck, so all he could do was wait for the mysterious owner to appear.

We later became friends, especially after he took John aside one day and confided to him that he found me *brave*, meaning "valiant, plucky" – a real compliment in French. As for driving in Paris, we both learned to enjoy it once the initial terror wore off. John and I soon mastered French traffic rules, including the fine points of driving L'Etoile, parking on the sidewalks, professing ignorance to *gendarmes* in our worst French and retrieving the car from the police pound (it's called a *fourière*).

Between shopping expeditions, I acted as overseer to the moving in and unpacking. This went ahead smoothly; my initial impression of the French workingman's competence and efficiency would be confirmed in later encounters. The apartment would need repainting and some decorating to restore it to its former elegance. (We wanted a background of the old France for modern, comfortable sofas.)

John had arranged for the first step in this transformation the month before, with the removal of worn carpet and the sanding and polishing of the parquet floors discovered beneath. Some light fixtures were missing – anything not included on the detailed list of improvements we had "bought" from the previous tenant, she had taken with her. But these were minor inconveniences. The kitchen was clean and well equipped – and surprisingly bright. It had a large double window giving a view of Paris chimneys and rooftops and their population of pigeons and cats.

The former tenant had installed an American refrigerator, large by French standards, and I had managed to stock it, make the beds and unpack the toys when John arrived a week later with the children – and some cash. (The bank had yet to approve our credit worthiness and grant us an account.)

They came on the same flight, Air France 004, John emerging from customs scowling with fatigue, Sarah and Nicholas bright with eager expectancy. (Nicholas wore his Christmas present of cowboy hat and holsters.) Two-year-old James arrived in France grinning like the Cheshire cat. Several hours earlier he had thrown a tantrum in the airplane and hurled food across the cabin. John and the stewardesses added tranquilizers to a glass of juice – knockout drops formulated for belligerents and drunks – that too he had thrown away in rage. But soon after he dozed off and slept like an angel the rest of the trip.

The first day of school for Sarah and Nicholas put a damper on the eager expectancy. The experience of entering a classroom in which you understand not one word is, for a child, like being dropped head first into icy water. Every afternoon I waited in the courtyard of the school with a crowd of other mothers, all jostling and shoving for a square foot of pavement and a view of their child descending the front stairs. (On rainy days, open umbrellas complicate this struggle for territory and viewing rights.)

When the children emerged, I could pick out Nicholas by his ashen face in a sea of bright ones. He met

one other English-speaking child in his class, a thin and scabrous little girl, and they clung to each other like waifs. It was several months before he learned enough French to begin enjoying himself, and not until the last of the year that he was able to profit from the instruction; but Sarah, with her flair for imitation, learned more quickly and was soon speaking a slurred and guttural Parisian slang that horrifies us.

I knew that Sarah understood French grammar the day she taught me to conjugate the F word in several tenses. Before he attained general fluency, Nicholas learned a string of swear words and scatological phrases – highly seamy and imaginative – thus qualifying for membership in one of several gangs or *bands* of playground boys.

With the noise and confusion caused by our moving in, it seemed a good idea to cultivate an alliance with the concierge of our building. A woman of my age, married to a policeman, she is uncharacteristically friendly and helpful, barring occasional lapses. These lapses can be explained by the noise she and her family must endure at night, living in a tiny apartment between two elevator shafts. She had worked in a factory until her two boys were born. In order to have more time with them she took a job as a concierge, even though in France the position of concierge occupies one of the lowest rungs on the social ladder, lower than a factory employee.

"I could pick out Nicholas by his ashen face in a sea of bright ones."

She loves children and happily looks after James when I need her. She is also a good cook, often filling the lobby and stairwells with the exquisite aroma of apricot tart. Early on she came upstairs to explain in a friendly way that the children should not be allowed to play on the landing. I had failed to reverse my standing orders from California days – that the boys go outside for shouting and wrestling matches.

But the noise did not provoke a reaction from our immediate neighbor until the day John decided to install and test our stereo system. A blast of the Jupiter Symphony brought an immediate phone call from Madame Dupuy, living just below us. After complimenting us on our taste in music, she launched a barrage of reproof on the amount of noise she had endured during our first weeks of tenancy, and her need, as a writer, for absolute silence.

How could she meet her next deadline with the cries of children, the vacuum cleaner on uncarpeted floors (when were we installing carpet?), the piano and now the stereo? I made a tactical decision to give her the bad news first – that we had no plans to carpet our parquet floors and that the children would begin piano lessons shortly. There followed several negotiating sessions, the first being tea in her apartment so I could hear the noise of little feet above. I agreed to limit the stereo, vacuum cleaner and piano to certain times of the day and proposed keeping closed the doors of our dining room, which lay directly above her study.

As our ESIK allowed us to have dinner in the kitchen, we used our formal dining room very little in the evenings, apparently the period of Madame Dupuy's greatest inspiration. We agreed to warn her ahead of time about dinner parties, and by inviting her to them occasionally, we turned the initial hostilities into a friendly if fragile truce.

Very soon after our arrival in Paris we became aware of our good fortune to have ended up in the 7th arrondissement. Most of the apartments we looked at were in the 16th, far from the center of things and considered *arriviste* by the discerning Frenchman. Here we were, through no effort of our own, living in the Faubourg St. Germain, a kind of village unto its own in the heart of Paris, avoided by bus and metro lines, unknown to most tourists.

Forays for food and supplies, and trips to the park soon acquainted us with this quiet and anachronistic neighborhood. More than any other arrondissement, the 7th abounds in *hôtels particuliers*. A walk past their open portals gives you a glimpse of eighteenth- and nineteenth-century France – great courtyards flanked on both sides by stables and servants quarters, and beyond the expanse of gravel the house itself, in unabashed, unembarrassed grandeur.

The reception rooms of these houses all face formal gardens in the rear and I've been told that a helicopter ride over the 7th arrondissement reveals that two-thirds of the area is green.

Many of these mansions have fallen into government hands and now serve as ministries or offices; others have been transformed into flats, those stables and servants quarters divided up into tiny studios and bachelor pads. Nevertheless, a walk in the 7th still gives you a flavor of Paris in its aristocratic heyday and in a few, a very few of those old mansions, life continues as before, with teams of servants to maintain the woodwork and furnishings dust-free, and Monsieur and Madame served with appropriate protocol. Our landlord has managed to maintain such a life in his *hôtel* on rue de Varenne. His is the largest privately owned garden in Paris, and rumor has it that he rides his horse there.

The residents of the seventh arrondisement today comprise the old and traditional bourgeoisie of France, a group that includes many artists, writers and eccentrics. They continue living their ordered and reclusive lives in spite of the incursions of bureaucrats and fastidious bachelors (living in those converted stables) and a fair number of foreigners like us.

One of the old *hôtels* in the neighborhood, the Hôtel Biron, now houses the Rodin Museum. It lies a five-minute walk from our apartment and, in the absence of a garden of our own, its great garden serves as play area for the children. It has a pond with ducks, long alleys for frisbee throwing, a sand box hidden in its depths, fences and statuary to climb (when the guard isn't looking) and wooded areas for hunting treasures – conkers, sticks, feathers, duck egg shells and wild strawberries.

Rue Barbet de Jouy is a quiet street of two blocks, having no shops but a fair number of official buildings – the ministries of Agriculture and Industry, the embassies of Sweden and Tunisia, the headquarters of the Paris Police and the residence of the Archbishop of Paris.

Recent troubles in Tunisia have earned for our street a twenty-four-hour armed police surveillance. When not on duty, these guards live in vans with surrounding movable barriers, in which they sleep, eat, play cards and ogle the passing ladies. The vans take up valuable parking space but on balance the residents welcome the presence of the guards. They peer into cars for evidence of bombs but must ignore parking violations and burglar alarms.

Our local shopping area lies on rue de Bourgogne which makes a climb perpendicular to the Seine between the Palais des Députés and rue de Varenne. There we find a small grocery store (you must walk sideways and very carefully between the shelves, so closely are they spaced), a fish market, an open-air vegetable market, two bakeries, two butcher shops, a shop that sells fine wine, smoked salmon and foie gras, a café, a tabac, four restaurants (two French, one Italian, one Vietnamese), a pharmacy, an art gallery, a shop that sells old tapestries, a shop with plumbing fixtures in the window, an Italian book shop and a French book store (which displays Madame Dupuy's histories), two gift shops, one of which specializes in shells and mineral specimens, a paper shop, two antiques dealers, a tanning salon, a studio where you can learn kung fu or tap dancing, and finally, at the bottom of the street, the shop of Monsieur Caro, the barber.

M. Caro's taste tends to the ultra-modern – pebbled walls and abstract paintings decorate this quiet salon – and his clients include many important persons from the nearby Palais des Députés. The soft-spoken M. Caro dresses entirely in black, as do the other barbers, and the female manicurist, young and slim, wears a tuxedo. I soon found out that M. Caro understood the word "short," so the two boys have become regular customers, emerging from his doors looking like little Marines.

"All the patrons of Euromarché, myself included, wear a grimace of impatience as they push their carts forward and sideways at the same time, to counteract the veer."

I came to France with great expectations of doing all my shopping at local shops, such as those along rue de Bourgogne, of adopting the customs of French housewives who stand in line at the butcher's and the bakery. I soon realized the futility of feeding a large family with daily shopping trips. Fruit alone disappears in our household at the rate of several pounds a day. The first time I went out to buy meat for the weekend, I stood behind two pert and impeccable ladies who ordered one pork chop and two small cutlets, respectively. They carried home their purchases in baskets. My order was for two large chickens and a dozen veal chops – I could hear the other clients snicker – for which I waited patiently while the butcher burned the remaining feathers off the chickens with his blow torch. No francophile would have envied me as I carried home the meat and my other purchases in plastic bags, draped over my arms and the stroller handles. The bags cut into my wrists and bumped against the stroller as I pushed James, a heavy child, up the narrow sidewalks of rue de Bourgogne. I had no free hand for an umbrella when it began to rain.

Thoroughly disillusioned, I decided to continue my once-a-week American supermarket habit, leaving the luxury of local shopping for the weekend's fresh vegetables. The nearest supermarket or *hypermarché* is a squat cement warehouse of a building on the outskirts of Paris.

As prelude to the week's shopping you must descend into a parking lot designed to give the modern consumer a preview of hell. I am sure the foul fiend lurks in the dimly lit recesses of the basement parking area at Euromarché. Water drips from overhead pipes and an enormous exhaust fan creates a roar and a wind throughout, to drown the sighs of the damned.

Conveyer belts carry you up to the main floor where you find ancient carts, one in twenty or so having a seat for a small child. These carts have braking attachments allowing you to take them down the conveyor belts to your car, a convenience I have found nowhere else in Paris. The drawback is that these attachments make the carts difficult to manoeuver – they tend to veer diabolically to the side. All the patrons of Euromarché, myself included, wear a grimace of impatience as they push their carts forward and sideways at the same time, to counteract the veer.

French apartments have high ceilings, finely decorated, but supermarket ceilings are lower than our own and are adorned with open conduits for pipes and wires.

And what is the shopper's reward for his visit to this paradigm of French modern architecture? Convenience and selection. He can fill his lurching grocery cart with everything from hardware to motor oil, clothing, books, toys, paper goods and liquor. There is a huge wine selection, three aisles of charcuterie, terrines and pâtés of all sorts, freshly baked bread, fish, live lobsters, meats, including horsemeat (already cut and packaged, no waiting for the butcher), fruits and vegetables from around the world, peanut butter and maple syrup, Asian ingredients but no Mexican (alas, no tortillas), and of course, hundreds of kinds of cheese. There are long lines at checkout, but once your turn arrives you must unload your cart (two in my case) as quickly as possible and bag your groceries yourself. (You bring your own bags for this or buy them there.) If you do not keep up with the checkout girl, whose only job is to check the groceries, you risk her displeasure.

I have become an expert at guiding two veering carts down the conveyor belts. Several employees stand there grim-faced to watch you as you descend, but no one offers to help you to your car. After loading the car myself I drive home, find a parking place near the service door (no trivial exercise), unload the groceries, carry them down the hall to the service elevator, load the elevator and take them up to the kitchen. This whole shopping trip takes a good three hours minimum. On Monday mornings, I do miss that prosaic piece of asphalt, the driveway, running alongside the kitchen door.

When you cannot keep up with the cashiers at the supermarket, they give you what we have come to call The Look. This is a studied air of disapproval, mouth pursed, eyelids lowered. The French are masters at it. (Nicholas observes that the French have big eyelids, very suitable for lowering.)

The ugly surroundings in which these poor girls work no doubt explain their surliness. To their credit, they always respond pleasantly to small talk and show some interest in the number of people I feed with two grocery carts of food each week.

But I cannot induce the sales girls in the paint section of Bon Marché, our local department store, to show any interest in me whatsoever. I have often found three of them huddled in conversation. When you ask for something, say sandpaper, one will wave her hand in the general direction saying, "Over there," giving you at the same time The Look for daring to interrupt their conversation. Fortunately I have discovered a small paint store whose proprietors, two brothers, love to talk to customers and will spend hours discussing politics with you while mixing up the right color of paint.

I encountered a prize example of this disdain for the customer or foreigner in late February when I took Sarah and Nicholas to the Louvre. I had by then reached the waddling stage of late pregnancy. At the coat check counter I asked where the bathrooms might be. "*Je ne peux pas vous dire,*" (I cannot tell you) the girl replied, giving me The Look. And where might I find out? She pointed up a long flight of marble stairs to a desk marked Information.

The girl watched me as I labored up the stairs, a child in each hand. The bathrooms, she informed me, were downstairs next to the coat check! When I passed the coat check lady on the way to the now-urgently-needed loo, I gave her The Look, but not a flicker of embarrassment shadowed her stolid, bureaucratic face. Obviously giving out information was somebody else's job, not hers.

It was not long after that Davidson Fallon came into the world. He was born at Clinique de la Muette, in the 16th, a new clinic, modern and clean. All went well, my doctor and his midwife happy to oblige me in what they no doubt recognized as a primitive local custom of Californians – the husband at the side of the mother during the birth.

It was after the birth that certain problems arose. I had brought my suitcase to the hospital, packed ahead of time and containing everything I had ever needed after the births of the previous three. But it had never occurred to me to pack soap and towel, greatly needed after labor. John had left before I discovered that the clinic did not possess these things. No amount of begging or pleading could persuade the nurses to find them for me – they simply did not have them. They finally came up with a bottle of anti-bacterial soap. For a towel I used my bathrobe.

Next problem: breakfast. For the exhausted and nursing mother of a newborn: one piece of baguette, one slice of butter and one cup of tea. I knew the futility of trying to drum up an egg or oatmeal, especially after my trouble with the soap, but I fortified myself with the hope of a more copious lunch. But lunch was a dieter's special: one slice roast beef (with *au jus*, as they say in America), a small serving of mashed potatoes, a wedge of cheese and an apple. "All our mothers are on a diet," the nurses explained. I realized I would starve to death if I stayed any longer and checked out, amid protests, that afternoon.

But not before a third problem presented itself, this one more difficult to solve. In France a baby must be registered at the mayor's office (every arrondissement has a mayor and a mayor's office) within twenty-four hours of his birth.

We volunteered my mother, then staying with us, for this task. The midwife had mentioned that we would need proof of marriage, so having left our marriage certificate in a file cabinet in our California garage we sent along my passport and John's and those of the three other children, convinced that the five passports all in the same name would satisfy the most skeptical bureaucrat.

At the mayor's office my mother fell upon a particularly unpleasant specimen of government worker who sent her away well chastised for daring to imagine that five passports could pass for a marriage certificate. The baby, she informed her, could not be registered without one.

That afternoon, after returning home, I consulted by phone with the midwife, who, it seemed, had the additional duty of following up on the registration of births. Suppose we just registered Davidson as illegitimate? "Horrors!" (In France probably so. Imagine having to suffer The Look at each and every contact with the French bureaucracy.) Maybe we should just not register him at all. "Oh Madame, this is not possible."

She would see what she could do and managed to obtain an extra twenty-four hours from the officials, during which time John got a notarized statement from the American Embassy stating that we were in fact married, and then return to the mayor's office, each step preceded by a long wait in line. We were beginning to understand why the French just roll their eyes when anyone mentions *l'administration française.*

If this incident had taken place several years earlier, we probably would have encountered trouble with the name as well. Until a couple of years ago the mayor's staff had lists of approved names and the authority to reject any name that didn't sound French, names like Barbara or Keith. The name Davidson would never have passed muster, although they might have made an exception for us as foreigners. I've been told that the reason for this complicated system of registration is to ensure that the father has the final say in the choice of the child's name.

In the end, Davidson received his birth certificate showing him to be well and truly the son of married parents; he also received his own *carnet de santé*, as do all other French children. This is a government-issued notebook showing the peculiarities of the baby's birth, and designed to give a running record of his growth, childhood illnesses and trips to the doctor and dentist for the rest of his earthly existence.

A French child needs this *carnet de santé* at various stages of his life, notably to enroll in school and to begin his military service. Doctors always ask to see a child's *carnet*, and they fill them out conscientiously. The French have not left the cataloging of a child's growth and illnesses to chance nor to the vagaries of a mother's impressions, but have instituted a comprehensive system of record-keeping administered by experts.

I now found myself trying to cope with four children – one of them very small – the daily drive to school (one hour round trip, morning and afternoon) and all the time-consuming chores of keeping a household in order. I needed, in a word, help, and that was when Madame Jamet entered our lives. John and I had decided that if we were to have a housekeeper, she should be French, so that the children and I would be exposed to French, not Spanish or Portuguese, throughout the day.

Central casting could not have sent us a more splendid example of the French housekeeper than our Madame Jamet, energetic in spite of her bulk, and meddlesome in the extreme. She had worked in *châteaux* and aristocratic households since the age of fourteen and was used to a strict division of labor among cook, maid, chambermaid, butler and nurse; and equally strict discipline of children.

Our noisy household and more relaxed methods took some adjusting to. On the plus side, the work is easier, no fine tablecloths to hand wash, starch and iron (a daily chore in former jobs) and no four-course lunches with all those dishes to wash. She confesses she finds me less demanding about things like dust and fingerprints than former employers.

Harder to accept is the fact that Madame doesn't seem to know her role; Madame Jamet cannot resist hen-pecking me about my proper duties as *Maitresse de Maison*. For example, Madame likes to enter the sacred preserve of the servants, the kitchen, and engage in improper activities, like cooking. What's more, unlike any of the cooks Madame Jamet has worked with, she allows the children into the kitchen at the same time, Davidson observing proceedings from his infant seat on the counter and James making a racket with the pots and pans. She hasn't hesitated to tell me that it's bad for her nerves, all this activity in a room that must double as her laundry room.

It has been difficult for Madame Jamet to get used to the fact that John doesn't come home for lunch (even though she doesn't miss the work involved). In her former households the lunchtime meal gave the day help a chance to slyly observe Monsieur and Madame together in case any cracks in the marital armor should appear. John's absence at lunch has led her to make the following underhanded compliment: "Your husband seems very nice, Madame, but of course it is hard to tell as I don't see him very often." Madame Jamet must content herself with having lunch with James and me, a necessarily uncomplicated affair. She says she finds Americans *simple*, a compliment in French, meaning "straightforward," "unaffected." But I suspect she misses those affectations that exercised her keen suspicions in French households.

In absence of chambermaid or cook for purposes of gossip and argument, Madame Jamet takes the occasion of lunch to talk to me. And what an awesome talent she has for talk! Words flow out in rivers, in torrents, phrase after phrase of idiomatic French. Each emphatic sentence she repeats several times, concluding these iterations with a loud guffaw. This guffaw is a signal to the brain, like Pavlov's bell, that it had absorbed the phraseology just heard and is ready for the next onslaught. *La méthode Jamet* far surpasses that of Berlitz and I find myself progressing effortlessly under her tutelage.

In September we enrolled James in a local public nursery school (more contact with *l'administration française*, this time complicated by the fact that James had no *carnet de santé*), and Madame Jamet's task is to take him there and pick him up. Off they trundle every morning, two spherical beings, one large and one small, their conversation focusing on the window cases of confectioners and pastry makers.

A less serious child than Nicholas, and younger, James' immersion into French has progressed without trauma. He has slipped into French as he would slip into a comfortable T-shirt. At first he mixed the two languages, giving us phrases like "*Je vais askée à Maman*" and "*Faut go pipi*," but as his vocabulary has expanded he scrambles less.

Running parallel to our adaptation to life in Paris has been the great project of undoing the experiments in decoration to which our apartment had been subjected. A team of painters soon gave us clean whites and soft pastels upstairs, eliminating, among other things, the cow spots. We painted out the black-lacquered walls of the entrance hall with something more cheerful. The living room, with its oak paneling, needed nothing, nor did the kitchen. That left two rooms on the main floor, the dining room with black ceiling and green fabric-covered walls (to match the billiard table), and a second salon, which the former tenant had transformed into a discothèque (more fabric on the walls, low false ceiling to accommodate speakers and a movie screen, shiny silver draperies and useless dim lights).

We had the false ceiling removed and the fabric with its plywood backing pulled off, making the happy discovery of more oak paneling beneath – but in very bad condition, full of holes and lacking chair rails and baseboards.

The French tell horrifying stories about remodeling, as do we, but a tip from John's office manager found us an excellent contractor. He brought in a team of carpenters, three mustachioed brothers who set up their saw in the middle of the dining room floor. In short order and with great skill, they filled the holes and repaired the baseboards. They reproduced the complicated chair railing and installed it with its many bevels. John, especially, was awestruck at the speed with which they worked.

The painters followed, and we soon had two splendid rooms, paneled and painted in pastels and white. Our initial good impression of the French craftsman was confirmed in our dealings with carpenters, plasterers and painters. They possessed not only efficient skill but also good taste and were only too willing to offer you their opinions on proportions, paint colors and drapery styles, not to mention the state of the French economy and the behavior of today's children.

Our apartment gives John plenty of opportunities to play the handyman, to *faire le bricolage*, a wonderful phrase denoting productive puttering. He has had to trade his well-equipped garage workshop in Los Angeles for a small cupboard, bursting with every tool he could possibly bring, and transformers to make them work. Most needed have been his talents as an electrician; the wiring system at number twenty-two is a nightmare of Cartesian logic, erratically applied by mad electricians using faulty materials. Lights go on and off mysteriously, and using more than two appliances running at once will blow the main fuse. Fifteen different kinds of light bulbs are required for the various fixtures – original Edison to ultra-modern – throughout the apartment.

The modern fixtures are recessed into our kitchen ceiling, which like the rest of the apartment is eighteen feet above the floor. To change them, John must stand on the very top step of a very tall ladder and reach up with both hands, one to turn the bulb and one to hold the rim of the fixture which has loosened since its installation several years ago. Plaster falling into the eyes adds danger and spice to this adventure.

As is customary in French apartments, we have access to two cellars or *caves* in the basement, one for storage and one for wine. We have the right to use two of the several maids' rooms or *chambres de bonne* on the seventh floor, dark and mean housing, with a bathroom down the hall, much sought after by students. (We have indulged in the illegal though widespread custom of renting them out.)

The apartment building has two elevators, a no-nonsense one serving the kitchen and seventh-floor rooms, and a lovely old-fashioned one serving the front door and lobby. This main elevator is a little wooden cage with paneling and grillwork. It has a pair of swinging doors that open inward. Then on each floor a heavy wrought iron door opens outward. And how marvelously quaint we thought our elevator, until the first time we tried to enter it with baby stroller and several packages. To enter you must hold the wrought iron door open with one foot, open the swinging doors with a push of the head, then quickly shove the stroller being careful not to catch the wheels (at this point you can forget the packages) – this manoeuvre requires all the patience and agility I can muster.

Once we loaded the elevator with suitcases, and then foolishly set James alone inside for the ride down. The suitcases fell forward, wedging the little doors shut and trapping James inside. Only after a great deal of pushing and prying did we manage to extricate the suitcases and the crying James. This incident happened in the early hours of the morning as we were leaving for vacation, to the delight, we assume, of our neighbors.

Aside from truculent elevators, the other obvious peculiarity of French apartments is their wealth of lockable doors, reflecting the French passion for privacy. Every room of our apartment has a thick door that can be locked with an old-fashioned key, behind which one imagines hushed affairs and whispered conversations. A corridor leading to two small bedrooms (presumably for baby and the nurse) has two doors to perform the double function of ensuring privacy for Monsieur and Madame and of protecting them

from noise. The main doors all have a complicated system of bolts and double locks to ward off thieves.

The passion for privacy is reflected in the telephone system as well. Ours is so contrived as to prevent anyone from listening in on you from another phone in the apartment. The phone bill comes as a lump sum, no listing of calls, not even long-distance ones, so that Madame will not be able to deduce whom Monsieur has been calling (or vice-versa).

Soon after David was born an accident gave us the opportunity to observe first-hand the French hospital system. Our apartment has a storage area accessible only by ladder, which the children had taken over as their fort. Sarah and a friend, Lisa, had decided to spend the night up there when Lisa, trying to descend without using the ladder, fell about eight feet, knocking herself unconscious.

These sorts of accidents never happen when it is convenient to attend to them and that night was no exception. John had just collapsed into bed after a long flight home from India, and I was still in that state of permanent fatigue that comes with nursing a baby on an hourly basis. We could not reach Lisa's parents so John pulled himself out of bed and drove

> *"The suitcases fell forward, wedging the little doors shut and trapping James inside."*

Lisa along with Sarah as interpreter to the nearest children's hospital, the Necker Clinic. This is a sprawling institution covering a large city block and having several entrances. The uninitiated must learn the hard way that each entrance corresponds to a different category of child, boys three to six for example, or infant girls. It took considerable time and several fruitless trips down dark alleys peopled with prostitutes and drunks before John found the entrance for ten-year-old girls. No parking lots, of course, but he found a spot on the sidewalk and carried in the injured Lisa, now conscious but delirious.

The next problem John had foreseen – the filling out of papers – although he had not imagined there would be so many. He and Sarah posed as Lisa's father and sister, thus avoiding delays. John pretended to be a fully vested member of the French social security system, filling in numbers at will. This got him past the front desk, staffed with listless attendants who showed no interest in checking the validity of the numbers or John's identification.

Next the trio was led down several long and dreary corridors, lit with single bulbs hanging from wires, to an emergency room staffed by a lone doctor. A button on his jacket said *En Grève,* meaning "On Strike," and he proceeded to explain to John in rapid French, Sarah translating, that it would not be possible to treat the child he held in his arms. John, now on the ragged edge of fatigue, had Sarah tell the reluctant physician that if he didn't treat his "daughter" immediately, someone else would need emergency treatment.

The look in John's eyes persuaded the doctor to relent and he began to see to Lisa with the proviso that he couldn't promise follow-up visits. (He didn't ask to see Lisa's *carnet de santé,* probably because he was on strike.) There followed tests and X-rays, Sarah describing the fall and giving a first rate showing of her skill in French. Lisa had suffered a mild concussion and a broken wrist and was confined to the hospital for several days. We left it to her grateful parents to sort out the papers John had so hurriedly filled in.

It has been immensely satisfying to observe the progress we have all made in French. I, of course, have learned French by osmosis, thanks to Madame Jamet. John speaks English at the office but on weekends he often visits that mecca of the home handyman, Bazaar Hôtel de Ville, a department store which dedicates the low-ceilinged catacombs of its basement to hardware of every sort. When he finds a salesman to help him locate some of the rarer light bulbs needed in our apartment, he chats him up and asks him the words for things like "hinge" (*un gond*) or "Phillips head screw" (*une vis cruciforme*).

By spring Nicholas and James had made enough progress to play on the sidewalk with other children, and nothing has delighted me more than to hear the boys biking and roller-skating in French, like real Parisian urchins. Madame Jamet, always one to take a pessimistic view of things, feels obliged to warn me that if I let the children play on the street, they will necessarily associate with the children of the street's concierges, something her previous employers would never have permitted. She is still adjusting to our American ways.

The American way of carpooling has not caught on among the French. I had harbored vain hopes of organizing one for *la Rentrée* – back to school – in September. Instead I find myself making the drive morning and afternoon. (We tried the Metro but that takes more time than the car.) What I lose in time

I am repaid in visual enjoyment, for our route takes us past many architectural marvels, backlit in winter by the fires and lights of sunrise and sunset.

As we leave our urban village of Faubourg St. Germain with its closely set buildings, we see the copper-domed complex of Les Invalides against the whole sky. When first built, this old soldiers' home stood in the middle of a cow pasture in a remote Parisian suburb. Over the centuries the city has grown up around it. Now flanked by elegant nineteenth-century apartments, and sharing the skyline with the Eiffel Tower, Les Invalides still looks down upon the largest open space in Paris, the Esplanade. Its alleys of trees shade countless old men playing *boules*, its grassy plots frame a wide boulevard ideal for prom-enades, pageants and parades, for official funerals and military displays, and for demonstrations both peaceful and violent, activities that frequently block traffic in all directions.

We cross the Seine on a more recent monument, Pont Alexandre III, a czar among bridges. Its cupids and winged horses welcome the lumpen motorist with imperial largesse and confidence. How beautifully its ornaments silhouette themselves against the sky. The children love crossing the Seine because it has boats – barges carrying coal and houseboats conking gently against the quais.

Once across the river we pass the Grand Palais, another monument reflecting the buoyant confidence of turn-of-the-century France. At rooftop level stand two splendid sculptures, the naked figure of a man on the south corner, a woman robed and majestic on the north, each in a chariot pulled by four plunging horses, a sight to kindle the soul on the greyest of mornings. When it rains, the verdigris of these bronzes glistens bright green against the dark sky.

As we cross the Champs-Elysées, the children take special delight in the vista of the Arc de Triomphe. On holidays, and when France greets officials from nations lesser than itself, the whole boulevard is fes-tooned with banners, and a huge tricolor swirls from the center of the arch.

Soon we find ourselves in the office district, bustling and crowded. Office workers in a hurry form clusters at the doorways of pastry shops for a quick breakfast of croissant or pastry. (An egg, I say, or the disdained oatmeal would put them in a better humor.) Further along we enter the residential district around Parc Monceau, with its fine collection of mansions and apartment buildings. Finally we arrive at the monumental iron gates and seething traffic jam in front of avenue Van Dyke.

Five large streets feed together in front of these gates; some drivers stop here in the middle of the intersection to let their children out of the car, thus impeding those hurrying to other destinations. There could not be more total confusion, more scowling and honking. In spite of the presence of two wardens to help at crosswalks, children dart between the cars like minnows among sharks. The school is at the end of avenue Van Dyke, housed in an old apartment building. At recess the children play under the mature trees and false architectural ruins of Parc Monceau – but they may not run on the grass.

We have had many welcome visits from friends this year who bring us items unavailable here, like parts for our American refrigerator. Canned pumpkin and cranberry sauce smuggled in on a 747 allowed us to have a traditional American Thanksgiving. (Our French guests had second helpings of everything.)

Christmas we will celebrate in the French manner, with champagne and foie gras from the little shop on rue de Bourgogne, no smuggling necessary. You can buy Christmas trees from the florist (no vacant lots in Paris) and the *Père Noël* visits all good children.

We extend warmest wishes to all our friends, French and American, for a merry Christmas and a happy 1984.

Sally

1984

This second letter from Paris I send as an established Parisian, caught up in the rhythm of life here – not the life of the student or the journalist, but as the mother of small children and an observer from the coach of daily routine. That routine still includes the drive each morning and afternoon to the children's school at Parc Monceau, which we now know in all its seasons, rich in banks of color in spring, lacy and spent in the fall; and the return home past the Grand Palais and over Pont Alexandre III. I continue to find inspiration in the apocalyptic horses dashing into the air from the roof of the Grand Palais and in the view of the Seine from the bridge, especially at cold winter sunrises, when the sky is Fragonard pink and mist lies upon the river.

The pleasure we take in Pont Alexandre III, ornamented to the hilt, surprises a French friend of mine, an artist, who read last year's letter. Critics and educators, she tells me, hold it up to their art students as an outstanding example of nineteenth century bad taste – overdone, pompous and sentimental.

"Critics and educators, consider Pont Alexandre III an outstanding example of nineteenth century bad taste – overdone, pompous and sentimental."

My routine still includes the weekly trek to the supermarket outside of Paris. No one can accuse the architects of Euromarché of sentimentality, having built an underground parking lot there of uncompromising bleakness. But during the summer holidays the management did try to brighten up the subterranean garage with gallons of red paint and posters for *haute cuisine* from the freezer section – salmon soufflé and veal with truffle sauce. They replaced worn-out fluorescents and repaired leaking overhead pipes, although exhaust fans still make a thunderous noise as before. The owners may have determined that their parking lot in its dark and derelict condition discouraged business; or perhaps the devil is out to enhance his image. The paint job has had the desired effect of attracting ever-bigger crowds as more and more French consumers enjoy the novel experience of buying shoelaces and Camembert from a single establishment.

Other changes have occurred in our neighborhood during the year. Skateboard windsurfing has become popular; on the Esplanade these cocky vessels tack and jibe their bright sails before the subdued tans of Les Invalides. One corner of the Esplanade, paved and balustraded, serves as a gathering place for youngsters on bikes and skates. A ramp has mysteriously appeared there, to facilitate stunts.

The twenty-four hour armed police guard on our street has disappeared, as have their two vans in which they endured the boredom of their watch with games of solitaire. This leaves the residents a good half dozen extra parking spots. (A new Minister of the Interior has moved police protection to those areas of Paris suffering from muggings and vandalism, leaving the embassies to fend for themselves.)

Several small shops have changed hands, giving Madame Jamet, our housekeeper, the opportunity to offer her opinions on the new proprietors. Monsieur Caro the barber has expanded his salon – more travertine and pebbled walls – and now serves ladies as well as gentlemen. Somehow the atmosphere is not the same as before, when the clientele consisted exclusively of men and the tuxedoed manicurist could devote her attention to ambassadors and government officials.

By now we know, or know of, most of our neighbors at 22, rue Barbet de Jouy. These include a French family that runs a painting restoration business in the apartment above us, a reclusive family rumored to be of the nobility, two American writers and a young Swedish concert pianist, Helge Antoni.

Helge rents two rooms in a back corridor of Madame Dupuy's, our neighbor just below. He and I have organized our lives to give her quiet in the afternoons when she writes. Helge practices in the mornings and late evenings, filling the lobby with strains of Mozart; the music travels up the pipes and late at night, when it's quiet, we pick up the subtle vibrations in the bedrooms on the third floor. When I mention this to Madame Dupuy she reminds me that the building is like a Swiss cheese and that she can hear every detail of our domestic life above her. Her latest book has appeared in the windows of local bookshops. Its subject: religious intolerance in the fifteenth century. She has shown exceptional, non-Gallic tolerance of us, her noisy neighbors, even with push toys, point shoes and games of fire engine with the vacuum cleaner on the parquet floors above her. Her patience is the more remarkable as the children's piano lessons have reached the Indian War Dance stage (*Danse Guerreuse Indienne*).

The boys have made friends with a pair of seven-year-old twins of Lebanese and American parents living in the second floor apartment at the back or garden side of the building. It takes several minutes to reach them by going out our front door, down our stairs and up theirs to their front door; but there is a constant to-ing and fro-ing of children, nannies, borrowed eggs and gossip through our kitchen doors, which are adjacent. This family has a butler, a maid, a cook and a nanny – the kind of team Madame Jamet worked with before she came to us.

The butler and the cook argue constantly – we can hear them when we open our kitchen window. Through their maid, Madame Jamet has learned all the details of this feud, as well as the guest lists of every dinner party. I detect a secret longing in her voice when she tells me about the counts and princesses who dine next door. Democracy may be fine for Americans but it lacks the drama and scandal that alleviated the tedium of countless generations of servants.

Madame Jamet also scavenges information from our concierge and so was able to tell me the fate of a Monsieur R***, living in the third floor apartment on the garden side of our building. He often invited young ladies to visit him at odd hours of the night. Sometimes these visitors, always new to the building, took the wrong staircase and knocked on our third-floor door instead of his.

Once this happened early, around nine o'clock, and our British baby-sitter, wholesome-looking and pretty, opened the door to find a bleached blond vision in boots and leather mini-skirt. Our sitter was wearing a white apron with ruffles on the shoulders and had at her feet three little boys in pajamas, all fresh from the bath, cheeks rosy and hair combed down. The girl looked horrified and hurried away to her expected assignment, one with a better pay scale than babysitting. Mr. R*** got his comeuppance this August when the concierge, hearing shouts, then gunshots, called the police. The gendarmes found no bodies but drugs and a cache of firearms in his apartment, and drove him away, sirens blaring. But he did not stay in jail for long, having friends in high places.

With another year in Paris, the children have made further improvements in French. Sarah's is the best, her accent and intonation perfect, and every sentence peppered with slang. The French student dialect is to standard French what Valley talk is to American English, a horrible perversion in the ears of most parents.

Nicholas and James understand almost everything now, although their French is not grammatically perfect. They make many small errors of gender and agreement; the French child also does this, to a lesser extent. They have French playmates and know all the names for marbles.

Davidson, now a toddler, speaks neither French nor English yet, but understands both languages. The French language is rich in adjectives to describe a child of this age – *turbulent, busculant, fatigant*. He has recently discovered the shower nozzles with flexible hoses, installed just at his level on the edge of the tub, as well as bidet plugs, which are easily removed and make perfect implements for banging against the paneling.

"Our sitter had at her feet three l ittle boys in pajamas, all fresh from the bath, cheeks rosy and hair combed down."

John's French gets a workout during expeditions for hardware items, including the little thing that holds a French window open about two inches (*un entrebâilleur de fenêtre* or "window-between-yawner"), or a cable with a rectangular nine-pin connector at one end and a round nine-pin at the other. (No succinct translation available, nor is the object.) He needed the latter item for his new toy, a computer, which he bought in American and smuggled into France in duffle bags.

It is a device with an infinite capacity to frustrate and cost money, especially when connected to our eccentric wiring system. He installed it in an empty linen closet and connected it to a plug on the opposite wall. This arrangement has offended Madame Jamet who believes the linen closet should be filled with fine linens, starched, carefully folded and stacked in neat piles. She refuses to heed John's warnings about unplugging the computer; so he often finds it unplugged and suffering from "surges."

John finds additional opportunities to exercise his French when he purchases software at one of several computer specialty houses in Paris. As most software has been developed in England or America, very little of it translated into French, the computer has acted as a port of entry for a great deal of the unwanted Franglais. Computer terms like *le software* and *le programmer* have infiltrated the French lexicon, joining other colorful émigrés from across the Channel and the Atlantic like *un bestseller, le profit and loss statement,* and the indispensable *weekend*.

My French has advanced beyond the textbook stage and I can now explain and complain, argue with taxi drivers and give orders to dogs and children in my second language. Even during aggravating moments – these happen frequently in Paris – I console myself with having added to my vocabulary words like body shop (*un atelier de carrosserie*) and tire jack (*un cric*), overdraft (*un découvert*) and spanking (*une fessée*), measles (*la rougeole*) and mumps (*les oreillons*). But I have yet to master that feat of French shopkeepers – the pronunciation of the phrase "*Bon jour, Monsieur and Madame*" all in one syllable.

As an adult, I can never hope to achieve the perfect accent that comes so naturally to the children, but I have made efforts to avoid sounding like an American. To do this you must pay careful attention to French intonation patterns. The French speak in mini-phrases, the voice lilting upwards at the end of each. (From a distance French conversation sounds chirrupy and melodious; English makes a low rumble.)

This upward lilting of the voice is more pronounced over the phone – the speed of the talk increases also. When Madame Dupuy calls to complain about the noise or Madame Rehaume calls from the bank, they speak in a racing singsong, a technique difficult to imitate. John survives well in face-to-face technical discussions but avoids the ordeal of speaking to a Frenchman on the phone.

> "*He has recently discovered the shower nozzles with flexible hoses, installed just at his level on the edge of the tub.*"

To speak like a Frenchman you must imitate his gestures. A forward thrust of the chin, for example, accompanied by lowering of the eyelids, indicates insouciance; two hands thrown up, palms forward, shows surprise. And there is that gesture of drivers – shoulders shrugged, hands flipped back with palms upwards, semi-sideways tilt of the head – a signal to surrounding drivers that they are all complete idiots. More than once I have been the recipient of this message.

It is James, age four, who excels at gestures showing enthusiasm, agitation and impatience. The French watch in fascination the typically French gestures rolling off his fat arms as French children in general have thin arms, more suitable to semaphore.

I gauge my progress in French at every meeting I have with two friends, Renée, a painter, and her daughter Florence, a writer. Both are vivacious and energetic; they speak a French that is rapid-fire, dizzying and breathless. With each meeting I come away having understood a fraction more.

Renée and her husband live in a wonderful light-filled apartment in the 8th. Her paintings, vigorous and bright, fill to the cornice the oval living room in which she entertains her many friends, including plenty of Americans. She finds in Americans an enthusiasm to match her own, as well as an appreciative market for her paintings.

Florence, an equally brilliant conversationalist, lives with her husband and four children in a crowded apartment in the Marais district. She and her family recently moved back into Paris from the country to take advantage of university-oriented public schools here. She has successfully juggled the upbringing of four children with a promising career as a writer, serving also as a advocate for women's rights in France.

The children are in evidence during her frequent gatherings of friends – writers, artists and lawyers – the French feminists' version of the salon. It was at Florence's that I met a lively and intelligent woman who had made a successful career as an astrologer to the wealthy and famous, after abandoning the less lucrative – and certainly less interesting – field of pharmacy.

French women maintain loyal friendships throughout their lives, but it isn't easy. They do not belong to the kind of charity groups that bring women together in America; nor do they play active roles in their children's schools – another avenue for contacts among American women. An American new to a neighborhood might expect to meet her neighbors at a block party or a gathering to honor newcomers, something unthinkable in France. The French themselves tell you they rarely know their neighbors in the same building even after living there for years. Americans drift away from high school and college friends, but the French, especially the women, keep these friendships for life, as new friendships after school days are difficult to establish. Meetings with friends must be arranged in advance – a visit to an exhibition or lunch in a bistro. Florence and I bought subscriptions for ourselves and our older children to a series of youth concerts to ensure that we would see each other often.

These concerts took place on Wednesday afternoons, a free afternoon for French children in private schools. Other days the children attend school from nine to four thirty, with one-and-one-half or even two hours for lunch, but little time at the end of the long day for lessons or activities. Children attending school near home return for lunch – you see them at noon and at two o'clock, carrying their heavy backpacks.

Sarah and Nicholas are *demi-pensionnaires*, which means they eat a hot lunch at school. (When questioned they admit to liking these meals, complaining only of one: sardines, eggs and spinach, sometimes served on Friday.) Their favorite is leg of lamb with lentils.

Public school children have the entire Wednesday free but must attend school on Saturday morning. Many French parents hope to see the private school schedule adopted in the public schools so they can have *un vrai week-end* as do the wealthy, and escape on Friday evenings to visit their property or their relatives in the country.

The school year begins in early September and runs to the end of June, leaving only two months for summer vacations. But students have a great deal of vacation throughout the year – a week at All Saints, two weeks at Christmas, a week or more during February, two weeks at Easter and numerous three-day weekends. (French governments have maintained the separation of church and state established during the Revolution but none has ever suggested eliminating holidays for saints' days or other religious festivals.) Even with their long day, French children attend school fewer hours per year than children from any other European country.

These days it is fashionable to complain about the decline of education in France. Sarah and Nicholas report that classrooms are often noisy and lacking discipline, but both bring home plenty of homework and the standards to us seem high. Sarah, now age eleven, entered the equivalent of sixth grade this year, a year that in France marks the end of primary school and the beginning of more serious studies.

The various subjects – French, English, science, math, history and geography – are taught by different teachers in one of two buildings separated by several blocks and a busy boulevard. As the children have no lockers, they must organize their backpacks each evening for the following day. At a meeting of parents last year, the headmistress urged parents to supervise the packing of books and notebooks for the next day's subjects.

Sarah's classes now end at differing hours, so she takes the city bus home from school, a novel experience for a California suburban child. She travels home with a pack of other children in uniform – blue jeans – all clowning and chattering their way across Paris to an audience of disapproving passengers.

> *"She makes her way on the bus to ballet lessons at Salle Pleyel."*

She makes her way on the bus to ballet lessons at Salle Pleyel, but we drive her to her Saturday riding lessons in the Bois de Boulogne. There she joins a dozen pre-teenage girls and one middle-aged gentleman for class in the covered ring. At one end of the ring, behind windows, parents watch from the tearoom and observation deck.

Riding instruction in France has suffered no decline in standards; the riding master tolerates neither noise nor mistakes; the girls accept his abuse without a murmur. The stables are architectural gems of variegated brick, reeking of turn-of-the-century gentility.

Nicholas, age seven, also has homework every night – reading in French and English, French spelling words to learn and, each week, a poem to memorize. He writes in handwriting (French children never learn printing) and must keep several tidy notebooks called variously *cahier de jour, cahier de roulement, cahier de poésie* and *cahier de mots*. Weather permitting, he spends his free Wednesday afternoons in the Rodin Museum garden, making arrows and tomahawks, finding hideouts and playing tricks on the warden.

James, now four, continues at the local public nursery school. These *écoles maternelles*, open to all children ages three to six, receive universal praise in France, in contrast to the rest of the educational system, which seems to please no one. James' school, hidden behind an austere wall on rue Janeau, has twenty or so brightly decorated classrooms and a dream playground, complete with tree house, round-about and a fleet of tricycles.

The teachers are uniformly patient and affectionate. Only the *directress* of the school doesn't smile, no doubt because she must spend most of her working hours seeing to it that her school's operations conform in every detail to the rigidities and rules of the French bureaucracy.

Madame Jamet still takes James to school and picks him up. This allows her to report to me, with magnification, any character defect the teachers may have found in our child. The French language contains no single-word translations for James' favorite activities – wiggle, kick, shout and scuffle; but the perfect word exists to describe his interest in food – *gourmand* – a passion he shares with Madame Jamet.

By now James can name every pastry the two of them see in display windows they pass on the way to school. They have become celebrities of sorts along the route. James says *bon jour* with a dimpled smile to everyone, and the pair stop for long discussions in front of shop displays, parked motorcycles and stray dogs and cats.

At home Madame Jamet continues to keep our apartment spotless with her mumbling and clucking ministrations, and to numb our brains with a constant stream of talk. Her moods change often, ranging from charming to disagreeable, and vaguely follow the rise and fall of the dollar. The slightest fall she announces triumphantly at the breakfast table, but passes over increases in silence. (Lately we haven't heard much about the dollar.)

This year two subjects have monopolized her thoughts – losing weight and winning the lottery. The diet began when she enrolled in a weight-loss program, much like Weight Watchers, with weekly weigh-ins and frequent visits with the doctors. She blossomed and basked in the attention and encouragement. At lunch, she weighed everything down to the last pea and prohibited me from preparing anything with butter. She began to slim down before our eyes. Every week she announced another kilo gone and at minus ten I paid her a thousand-franc bonus to encourage her to continue (worth just over one hundred dollars at the time). But somewhere around minus thirteen things got vague – less frequent announcements, missed appointments for the weigh-in. We began to hear crackling sounds from her hand bag again – pastry wrappers. The vanished kilos quckly reappeared, and that was the last we heard of the diet.

Meanwhile one of her friends won the *grand loto*, the sweepstakes in the national lottery. Both the friend and her husband worked in a factory and earned the minimum wage. With their winnings they bought an apartment in Paris with a room for each of their two children and built themselves a house in the country. (The dream of all Parisians is a house in the country, whether a chateau requiring constant maintenance or a mobile home in a trailer park, for which they will willingly sit for hours in heavy traffic on weekends.)

The success of her friend has set Madame Jamet dreaming of victory in the *loto*. She purchases one ticket a week and knows exactly what she would do if she won: quit work, outfit her ample figure at Dior and Balmain, have her hair done weekly at Chez Alexandre, visit friends and play bridge.

Madame Jamet's presence allows us to observe at close hand a particularly splendid specimen of that species called the French and to make certain generalizations about the French national character. The French are artists in their work and excel in carrying out a preordained task in a careful manner. Madame Jamet is an expert at stretching a simple ten-minute job into a two-hour masterpiece of French craftsmanship and expertise. The laundry, for example, ends up in piles and piles of fussed over, perfectly ironed, artistically folded clothing, gracing the kitchen like statutes in a sculptor's studio. It has taken me a long time to convince her that some things – like old pajamas, now on their fourth child and missing the feet – don't need ironing. She protests that without proper ironing and folding, the pajamas, under-wear and socks will not stay in neat piles.

In the old days everyone from the street sweeper to the nobleman did the kind of work or non-work proper to his station, and neither the French Revolution nor the pervasive influence of America has changed this tendency to compartmentalize work. Once I asked Madame Jamet to polish the knob on the outside of our entry door and she exploded with indignation – that was the concierge's job. (She was happy to polish the identical knob on the inside of the door.)

In the department stores the sales girls can help you (they don't always) but another category of employee takes your money; in the supermarket the *caissières* check your groceries but do not weigh them. This means there are always lines in the produce department where special employees weigh your fruits and vegetables. (Some stores have recently installed machines that allow you to weigh and label your vegetables yourself, thus condemning to redundancy a whole category of employee.)

To the American businessman working in France, the office worker, though skillful, seems to lack enthusiasm and initiative. The secretary will type and take shorthand but won't run errands or stand in for the receptionist; the lowest office employees grumble at having to make the coffee because no one above them will do it. In general, the French office worker does his task well but never more than asked. He sees himself as an individual, not as a member of a team, and is ever alert for injustices to himself and special treatment for others in the land of liberty, equality and fraternity.

The French are strong in logic and tend to apply abstract categorizations to all activities of life. This was brought home to me one day when I bought a new broom – an ordinary straw broom – and began to use it on the kitchen floor. Madame Jamet corrected me in the nick of time. The broom I was about to use was a terrace broom, not suitable for the kitchen floor.

Madame Jamet then gave me a lesson on brooms. A kitchen broom is a light-weight push broom having fine hairs – not to be confused with a parquet broom, also a push broom but finer-haired than its brother in the kitchen. Every type of floor demands a different type of broom – what could be more obvious? – and mixing them disturbed her sense of logic and equilibrium, even after I pointed out that the lowly terrace broom did a better job of removing dirt from the corners.

The street sweepers in Paris have their own design of broom. It looks like a bunch of twigs, tied together by hand and bent in one direction, apparently due to the action of pushing water along the gutter. A closer look reveals the twigs to be plastic, so somewhere in France a factory turns out thousands of street sweeper brooms, pre-bent and designed to resemble the hand-made products of peasants. In every corner of France the broom world hierarchy is thus maintained, from the common street broom to the parquet aristocrat.

The French may be slow to adopt new ideas, but once they do they make them part of their tradition. One hundred years ago they considered cheese a peasant food. However it was that cheese became a part of the haute cuisine tradition – perhaps introduced by an enterprising restaurateur, or first served by an eccentric hostess – the cheese course is now a tradition rigidly practiced and considered typically French.

Being artistic and meticulous, the French will carry out a fixed idea in a fixed way over centuries. Until its revision a few years ago, *La Cuisine de Madame St. Ange*, the French equivalent of *The Joy of Cooking*, instructed the housewife on the size and shape of the basket she must carry when doing her morning errands.

The patient follow-through of a fixed idea has had happy results in the area of architecture. For example, to the French way of thinking a town house or apartment building must have a certain regular shape, large windows, carefully constructed doorways and must of necessity be ornamented – but no overly so – with details in wrought iron, brick and stone. The implementation of this formula, allowing for variations of style within a narrow range, may have been mindless, but over the centuries it has resulted in the most uniformly beautiful city in the world. (Strict height limitations, and a man named Hausseman, also contributed to the successful results.)

Towards the end of the last century French architects broke with the narrow limitations of these standards, producing buildings at once fanciful and ponderous, like the Grand Palais. The reaction to this bourgeois sentimentality can be seen in today's modern architecture which breaks with all traditions, including the tradition of good craftsmanship.

It is not always easy for children living in the most uniformly beautiful city in the world. The great majority of French children live in apartments and must conform to certain standards of behavior, summed up in the term *bien-élevé* or "well-brought-up." This is the greatest compliment you can pay the parents of a French child, that their child is *bien-élevé*, meaning that his behavior is compatible with antique furniture and octogenarian neighbors living in the same building. Needless to say, our boys' wrestling matches and baseball slides on waxed floors (whether in the apartment lobby or at the Louvre) do not conform to the ideal of *bien-élevé*. The American will find something to praise in the unruly youngster, his curiosity or creativity; the Frenchman wastes no compliments on the badly behaved child.

The French child has few places to let off steam. The furniture in his apartment is either meager or uncomfortable, and he cannot run on the grass in the parks. There are no playing fields in Paris, even at the largest schools; this, along with the French preference for individual sports, hinders the widespread organization of team sports for children. Some enlightened parents recognize team sports as an important character-building tool, and lately the government has talked of mandating daily physical education and sports in the French schools, but they have not yet told anyone just where these activities would take place.

As I mentioned in last year's letter, we allow our boys to let off steam by riding or skating on the sidewalks, a practice that causes many raised eyebrows. One friend, intelligent and open-minded, was shocked, painfully so, that we, living in an apartment with eighteen-foot ceilings, allowed our children to play on the sidewalk with the children of the concierge.

Like many Frenchmen, he admires from afar the social mobility found in America; but centuries of class-consciousness militate against putting democratic ideals into practice in France. And to be fair, in very few American neighborhoods do you find the rich and the poor living in close proximity as you do in French apartment buildings, with families of immigrants crowding the seventh-floor *chambres de bonne* and wealthy, even aristocratic families living in the largest of the apartments.

Homework keeps Nicholas from spending as much time on the sidewalk as he would like. He is required to read aloud to me every evening, and this we do with a dictionary in hand. As a former reading teacher, I take great interest in the methodology and subject matter of his reading book.

The French language is more phonetically regular than English (in spite of the fact that half of the letters aren't pronounced) and this lends itself to a theoretical approach to the teaching of reading. The American reading book tries to seduce the young reader with stories and colored pictures starting on page one, but the French reader introduces all the sounds, one by one, with sentences containing words to illustrate those sounds, before making any attempt to tell a story – just as in former times music teachers gave their students scales and chords before allowing them to play any songs. Some of the illustrative sentences are just that – illustrative of the sound just introduced and theoretically correct, without making sense to children. Some are even unsuitable for children. Thus we read in the chapter on the letter F, "*Sophie a le coeur fatigué, elle ne peut pas courir.*" "Sophie has a tired heart and cannot run," – hardly a cheerful thought for a youngster of six years.

The French love children, especially the *bien-élevé* variety, but don't believe in protecting them from the realities of life. In his first handwriting notebook Nicholas had to copy the phrase "*Le clochard est sur le banc,*" – "the tramp is on the bench" – next to which he drew a bearded stick figure lying on a park bench.

And what were we to make of the following sentence found in the lesson on the letter H? *Katherine a mis le haricot sur la mousse humide,*" which I translated as "Katherine put the bean on the wet mousse." We had already observed that the French, even the children, take more interest in food than their Anglo-Saxon counterparts, but this sentence left us dumbfounded.

Why, we asked ourselves, was the mousse called wet? Chocolate mousse, the mousse preferred by children, may be moist but no one would call it wet. In a cooking class (yes, I have a little time for things like that now) we made *mousse de poisson, sauce écrivisse*. It was delicious but I shouldn't think to call it wet. And would the *bien-élevé* Katherine dare to put a bean on it, assuming the unlikely case that wet mousse and beans were served up together? Thoroughly mystified, we presented this puzzle to a French friend who explained that the word *mousse* also means moss, in which case, he assured us, the sentence made perfect sense. Certainly Katherine's reputation as a well-brought-up child was saved, but the image of her in the woods, carefully placing her lone bean on the north side of a tree, brought us no closer to solving the mystery.

The French love to eat, and the fascination with food extends to children. In Nicholas' reading book we find food mentioned on almost every page. We learn that celery tastes good with mayonnaise, for example, and that Alice likes *escalopes* with lemon sauce. One boy looks forward to a family meal of leg of lamb, wild mushrooms, cheese and oranges, but his sister, who is dieting, gets only soup; another child describes dinner at his grandmother's house – shrimp, tomato salad, veal cutlet, fried potatoes, Camembert cheese and cakes with jam.

Our children would not have eaten the shrimp, the tomatoes or the Camembert, as they would also refuse eggs in aspic, a gelatinous dish the French child anticipates with relish.

In another book we find a dialogue between two hungry dogs, deep in discussion on the merits of garlic in sausage, when the cat runs off with their piece of roast beef.

In spite of the interest shown in food, owners of small restaurants and cafés complain of changing French eating habits. A few years ago the humblest workman took his lunch leisurely in a café, with starter, main course, cheese, dessert and wine. Today the typical lunch comes increasingly in the form of a sandwich. Paris has sadly watched the proliferation of fast food outlets to cater to the poor, the hip and the hurried.

Fortunately, fast food habits have made few inroads in that tenacious French tradition – the Sunday midday meal. I felt it only fair to our beautiful dining room, with its paneling, marble fireplace and lofty ceiling, to adopt the custom in our family. The children seem to enjoy the adventure in formal eating, especially when John ventures into the kitchen beforehand to produce French fries in our built-in deep fat fryer.

After the meal, John has his Sunday nap, the older children run off to the park (assuming it isn't raining) and Davidson and I bundle up for a walk. First stop: our *vestiaire*, the large coat closet found in all French apartments, often behind curtains instead of a door. Usually an artistic jumble of coats, umbrellas and hats, the vestiaire sometimes serves as subject matter for painters. Ours contains, in addition to jackets, coats, scarves and mittens, roller skates, toys for the sandbox, briefcases, duffle bags, children's push toys and school backpacks.

Coats on and Davidson in hand, we exit by the service or kitchen door, as we now keep his stroller just inside the service entrance. (This at the suggestion of our concierge, who no doubt grew tired of hearing us struggle to get the stroller in the main elevator.) So instead of taking the main elevator, as would be proper, we descend the back stairwell on the service one.

Here I must interject a few words about French elevators in general – in last year's letter it was the paragraph on elevators that brought the most comments from our friends in France. My friend Florence confesses that the struggle with the stroller and Parisian elevators drove her to move to the country when her children were small. Renée says she remembers that some pre-war elevators had cords instead of buttons, which you had to pull at just the right moment to stop at the desired floor.

The children would have loved the cords and fighting over the right to pull them. Between our apartment door and our car in the underground garage across the street there are nine buttons for elevators, doors or lights, and when we first arrived in France the children fought at each one for the right to push it.

Once this year Sarah visited a classmate who lived in a remodeled building. Its elevator was an exact replica of our own, only renovated – wood refinished, brass polished and all three doors (heavy outer door and two inner doors) equipped with heavily loaded springs. It was a terrifying experience getting in and out of the thing; you needed four hands, all free, to prevent a fatal blow by any one of the three doors banging shut.

Our service elevator lacks the charm of the main one but it is equally difficult to enter. It has an inner and an outer door, both of accordion iron, which open by sliding to the left. The difference is that the outer door stays open while the inner door must be held with one hand or propped. Once in you must continue holding open the inner door while you slide shut the outer door with your other free hand; and this is the elevator we must use for bringing up heavy packages and taking down the trash.

With Davidson strapped safely in his stroller we exit number twenty-two by the service door and turn left, taking rue Barbet de Jouy south towards rue de Babylone. As it is Sunday, a day of rest for Parisian street cleaners, there are many visual reminders upon the sidewalks of the large dog population in Paris – one-and-one-half million of them in a city of four million people.

In France every aspect of life is touched by the government, every possible item taxed or licensed – except for dogs. No politician would dare risk the loss of votes he would incur by proposing any sort of control on them. The French will be the last people on earth to adopt the pooper-scooper.

Cleaning up after dogs is the mayor of Paris's number one headache. Monsieur Chirac has instituted a brigade of lime-green-and-white, sidewalk-suitable motorcycles driven by young men in matching lime-green jumpsuits. The back end of the scooter lowers onto the offending pile, brushes it into a tank of antiseptic fluid and scrubs the soiled spot. (I once saw the whole cavalcade of green and white parading up the Esplanade des Invalides, proving the French talent for making a pageant of anything.) But the labor of the jumpsuited scooter men is the labor of Sisyphus; the dogs soon return to exercise their sacred right to foul the sidewalks.

John has his own method for dealing with dogs. Once when leaving our building he found a dog squatting in front of the apartment door, not two feet from the gutter where it could have gone with equal ease – but perhaps its chicly dressed owner wanted to spare her pet the discomfort of getting its feet wet. John gave the dog a mighty kick, thereby winning the permanent admiration of our concierge, who was there to see the incident.

Today we shall stroll – carefully – along rue de Babylone, which offers us a second local shopping area. Although not as complete as that of as rue de Bourgogne, it contains many interesting shops, including a shop that sells second-hand designer clothes and a bakery with dough sculptures of turtles and alligators in the window. A paper store, with plastic smurfs and matchbox cars in the display, child level, marks the border of the boys' roaming territory. Nicholas and James are allowed to come this far to gaze at the collection of toys and spend their allowance on the difficult choice.

At the corner of rue de Babylone and rue Barbet de Jouy is a *brasserie* or bar with large windows, the kind found everywhere in France, with standard-issue awnings, tables, chairs and coffee maker. On weekdays businessmen in suits play the pinball machines there and workmen in coveralls take an early-morning nip of eau de vie.

Across the street is the Pagoda Theatre, a replica of a Chinese pagoda house built by the original owner of Bon Marché department store. For many years this building was hidden behind a high wall and few Parisians knew of its existence. Its present owners have removed the wall, revealing the unusual structure with its Chinese garden, weeping willow and pond. Today it serves as a teahouse and movie theatre.

We take rue de Babylone east, towards rue du Bac. On our right is a long wall, behind which lies a huge garden, once belonging to the local convent. On this land, some of the most expensive real estate in the world, the nuns raised raspberries and lettuces for their hospital patients. A few years back, after a long court fight to keep the land out of the hands of developers, they gave half the garden to the city of Paris to use as a park.

The city fathers transformed the raspberry patches into a play area designed with children in mind, with climbing frame, sandpit, slide and, best of all, grass that can be walked upon, sat upon, played upon. This is one of the few parks in Paris to allow invasion of the sacred grass, and I have noticed that the lawn here survives as well as elsewhere.

In warmer months the park is always crowded with children and sunbathers of all ages. During the August calm, the *gardiens* install an inflated pool and stand back to supervise water fights and splashing.

The government has shown less wisdom, less bourgeois sentimentality, in its development of another garden, immediately across the street from this park. They have hidden it from pedestrian view by an ugly concrete structure, purpose unknown, this in the Faubourg St. Germain where modern structures are supposedly forbidden.

But the view straight ahead is a nice one, the variegated walls of rue de Babylone leading the eye to the turreted corners of Bon Marché. At the end of rue de Babylone we pass several religious bookstores – I wonder whether the irony of selling religious books on rue de Babylone occurs to any of the proprietors? (The center for foreign missionaries is located in this section of Paris, along with several convents and a monastery.)

At the corner of rue de Babylone and rue du Bac lies Sarah's favorite store, Bon Marché, the city's first *grand magasin* or department store, long since past its prime but still a source of housewares, hardware, children's clothes and exotic groceries. In former times the store dedicated a whole department to nuns' habits and priests' robes. This has now disappeared, as has the department that sold uniforms for butlers and chambermaids. Instead the store displays lacy lingerie in the windows by the front door and in the area just inside. You can find a department that sells square polyester dresses – yes, French women do gain weight when they reach a certain age – on the third floor.

Sarah knows Bon Marché from top to bottom, haunting it frequently after school, especially the stationery department where she spends her money on things she insists she needs, erasers smelling of banana esters, tasseled pencils, rubber bracelets and notebooks of every size and description.

We turn left on rue du Bac and walk towards the river, passing a variety of shops selling antiques, Chinese porcelain, leather goods, old dolls and Italian groceries. Our favorite shop in Paris is Deyrolle at number forty-six, recognizable by its window display of taxidermy specimens. Upstairs is a labyrinth of rooms containing treasures from the natural world – rock and shell samples, mineral rarities, skeletons, stuffed animals, fossils, butterflies and beetles impaled on cards – everything dusted and cosseted by a team of white-coated salesmen who speak only in whispers. If your favorite dog dies, Deyrolle will discreetly have it stuffed for you.

We now double back and return along rue de Grenelle, a narrow street of apartment buildings and *hôtels particuliers*. They keep the street in perpetual shade, blocking out all but a jagged ribbon of sky. The sportsman, the Texan, spoiled by open spaces, wonders how people can live in the sunless lower floors. As it is Sunday, the street is quiet, but behind curtains and shutters you can hear the sounds of Parisians in voluntary confinement – someone watering plants, playing the piano; the conversations of families at dinner, clinking plates, running faucets, the easy noises of a Sunday afternoon as thousands of Frenchmen find comfort in their Sunday roast and bottle of wine.

Just before rue de Bourgogne, we turn right and circle around the Basilique Ste. Clotilde. It was long a mystery to me that I could not find this miniature Gothic cathedral listed in any guidebook, even though its twin towers form an important element of the Left Bank skyline. The reason, I eventually learned, is that the church is a nineteenth century copy containing nothing original. (The despised nineteenth century again.)

Nevertheless, it is a very good copy and its interior, uncluttered by souvenir stands, swarms of tourists or Rococo additions, gives a better impression of a medieval cathedral than the highly visited originals. It also has a wonderful organ, and the church has attracted organists from around the world, including César Franck.

It's time to turn homeward and to bid you good-bye, but not before telling you that we finally solved the mystery of Katherine and her bean. French children used to bring home sphagnum moss and set it on the radiator. They would moisten it, set a bean on it, and watch the bean grow and sprout. Today children use cotton rather than moss and the custom seems to be dying out altogether.

From the City of Light, we send you best wishes for Christmas and the New Year.

Sally

1985

n June of this year our sojourn in Paris came to an end and we returned – regretfully – to California; but our two-and-one-half years there gave us time to know her in all her moods and seasons.

The year begins in September with the great return – *la rentrée* – the return of Parisians to their city of delights and aggravations. The first aggravation is heavy traffic on the autoroutes that bring them home; but Paris puts on her best weather for the homecomers, blue skies and warm days, as they take up jobs, school and routine. Shorts and sandals give way to suits and leather shoes, the kind of tailored clothing in which the Parisian, though he may say otherwise, feels most comfortable; but the summer tan, that great status symbol, lingers for some time.

La rentrée means that after the August calm the shops reopen, the department stores draw crowds, the cafés fill up and the traffic becomes unbearable. Students and newcomers search out part-time jobs and rented rooms, both in perpetual short supply; youngsters return to school with heavy backpacks; and the moneyed classes begin a new round of theater-going, parties, receptions and affairs . . . in short, life in Paris begins again with all its pattern, urgency, protocol and intrigue.

With any luck, the good weather holds for several weeks. A northern city, Paris bathes for long hours in reddish evening light. She has inspired the painter at all times of the year but never more than in autumn when that slanting light, filtered through a thin haze, casts its magical influence on turning leaves, on the rippling Seine, on crowds, on sculpture and ironwork.

The artist best captures this effect, ephemeral and dreamy, with the inspired daubing of the Impressionist, rather than with line or shape; but later in November, when the leaves have fallen and the outlines of the city's buildings, noble and pompous, reveal themselves, Paris becomes a city of bold shapes and interesting spaces. Paris in late fall inspires the etching and the engraving.

The indigo sky of these clear evenings provides a most perfect and decorous background for the pastel ochres of Parisian limestone. One such evening last fall, when the air was still and warm, a full moon rose to silver Notre Dame, the Hôtel de Ville and all the glorious company of spires and domes and mansard roofs. Naturally the bridges and boulevards were jammed, all Parisians – the denizens of garrets, the citizens of worldly *salons* – out to admire their city in her most seductive, most gracious of moods.

Winter sets in with plenty of soggy days and grey skies, but the size of sidewalk crowds hardly diminishes; the pedestrian only bundles up and walks more briskly. When vendors selling hot crêpes and chestnuts appear, we know that Christmas is imminent; decorations soon follow. The Champs-Elysées becomes a fairyland of tiny lights, leading in a graceful curve to the Arc de Triomphe. The big couturier houses – Dior, Balmain, Chanel – festoon their windows with garlands and ribbons. Over Rue Royale are posted huge, rigid cutouts of antique cars or hot air balloons, appealing to the shopper through nostalgia for earlier decades. The merchants of Avenue George V celebrate the buying season by hanging over their street a banner of lights announcing . . . Avenue George V.

The department stores of the Opera district canopy Boulevard Hausseman with space-age decorations; huge tinsel forms, turning spirals, shooting stars and zigzagging neon lights to distract the motorist. Shoppers jostle for front views of the window displays – Lego cities with moving trains or toy monkeys swinging from artificial trees.

Christmas is a family holiday in France, celebrated at mass and at Christmas dinner, all generations in attendance; but New Year's Eve the Parisian celebrates with friends, eating oysters and drinking champagne. It is one of two nights of the year when the law allows you to make as much noise as you like, the other being Bastille Day, July Fourteenth.

In the new year, children eat *galettes des Rois* in honor of the three kings. This delicious concoction of puff pastry and almond paste may hide a coin or favor. The child who finds it wins the little paper crown the pastry-maker slips into the bag along with the *galette*.

Lively street life continues in neighborhood shopping areas, even after the holiday season. The cold and dark of winter evenings foster a sense of camaraderie among shoppers, who run their errands and buy groceries and flowers on return from work. Each little shop is an island of light in the dark; within, the shopkeeper greets you with his high-pitched salutation. The open-air vegetable markets tent the front of their stalls with clear plastic, and in their steamy interiors you can buy lettuce from Portugal or fruit from Gambia and Senegal.

Under the streetlights pass the silhouettes of dark-coated shoppers, their heads wreathed in frosty breath. Laden with packages, with baskets of fare from exotic places, each struggles momentarily with a heavy building door before disappearing inside.

Winter weekends bring on bouts of cabin fever, especially for those like ourselves who lack property in the country to tempt us onto the highways, and who have small children to limit excursions. In all but the worst weather, desperate parents send their children off to the park, granny or nanny chaperoning the youngest. (While visiting last winter, the children's paternal grandmother took them to the Luxembourg Gardens, where she partook of a local custom – fighting with other grandmothers for places on the merry-go-round.)

But the number-one activity of the long winter weekend is movie-going. Parisians average more movies per year than any other city-dwellers. At any given time, over one hundred movies are showing in Paris, everything from oldies to avant-garde, and always plenty of children's movies. One theater near L'Etoile shows only Walt Disney movies, and during our stay in Paris the children and I probably saw every movie Disney ever made.

France has a rating system for movies similar to America's, but advertisements shown before each film fall outside the censors' jurisdiction. You might choose a movie suitable for young eyes and ears – say, *The Black Stallion* or *Man Among the Wolves* – but before the movie starts you must endure half an hour's worth of ads for stockings (crowds of men following the swaying derriere of a mini-skirted girl in red fishnets); underwear (returning home after a long day's travel, girl embraces boy and removes, not her shoes, but her blouse, to reveal the bra to which she owes it all – youth, beauty, fame and success); and sportswear (huge python wraps itself around the nude torso of a girl in an appeal to buy the particular brand of designer jeans she is wearing).

Dancers in war paint, gyrating to hard rock and neon lights, bid the viewer to indulge in popsicles and Perrier. Only in the ads for McDonald's do the actors wear conventional clothes, have clean-cut hairdos and look normal. They sing the McDonald's song in French and flash smiles brimming with innocence and youth.

Children are prohibited from viewing X-rated movies, but while standing in line for something suitable they can see the posters for these movies – a naked woman screaming about something or other, a couple in exotic embrace, etc., these same posters lifted high up on the marquettes of the Champs-Elysées. The Frenchman, exposed to nudity on poster and celluloid from an early age, is blasé to these displays, but the American is amused, embarrassed, nonplussed.

I remember a poster-sized advertisement that appeared throughout Paris last year. It showed a man, bronzed and naked, diving off a diving board. His hands in front of him, he was horizontal in the air. The children pointed out that the normal man, under normal conditions of gravity, would have certain things hanging down. This Frenchman lacked vital parts. I hope it was the airbrush or surgical tape that contributed to his neutered condition, rather than more drastic measures. I cannot remember, or begin to imagine, the product he was peddling.

The Frenchman clothed reveals far more about himself than the Frenchman naked, and the Sunday afternoon fashion show on the Champs-Elysées provides diversion more entertaining than any movie. You must try for a sidewalk or window seat in one of the cafés for the best view of this parade.

Observe the apparel of skinheads and aristocrats. Every imaginable fashion struts before your eyes – black leather jumpsuits, tailored couturier clothes, furs chic and shaggy, western clothes, fluorescent clothes, adolescent clothes, Indian saris and Arab gowns. The young favor sweatshirts that say UCLA or Detroit Tigers. (These are very "in," you can buy them in the supermarkets.)

Couples of all sorts join the parade, tweeded and blue-rinsed representatives of the bourgeoisie, old men with young mistresses, fashionable pairs showing hours of preening and others looking deliberately of just emerging from torrid sheets. Crowding the sidewalks and cafés and movie houses are gangs of teenagers, tourists by twos and threes, country bumpkins, visiting rugby players in kilts. . . and beggars. Mimes and magicians in costume play to captive audiences in the movie lines.

Winter lasts a long time in Paris. The more fortunate vacation in Morocco or Crete and maintain their tans in the many tanning parlors found throughout the city. But for the most part, come February, Parisians look pale, peaked, pinched, hollow-eyed and weary. Ah, but spring is just around the corner, only a few weeks away. The rain provides the clue. It always rains as the weather warms up. It rains every day now, drizzling rain or pelting rain. Attendance at old and obscure children's films goes up, as every child has seen the new releases.

Every year at this time, rain notwithstanding, Paris suffers the infestation of *Homo vacaciones*. The natural habitat and circumstances of these creatures vary, but during this migratory season they fall into two distinct categories. The parka subspecies is brightly colored and highly peripatetic, thanks to its footwear (tennis shoes). Its eating habits are simple, and it often carries several days' nourishment in a dorsal protuberance or "backpack." Male and female of the parka subspecies are indistinguishable to all but the most expert observers.

The trench coat subspecies has more drab coloring, usually beige, although hardy black variants have been spotted. The female can be distinguished from the male by thicker and more bouffant head plumage. This group lacks the dorsal protuberance, but the male will often carry photographic equipment. They tend to travel in large buses from which they emerge at feeding times. The period of tourist infestation lasts until late November.

The Parisian has learned to ignore the tourist. As buds appear on the trees, his thoughts focus on the coming of spring. The rain continues. Soon Paris is leafy and green but skies are leaden. Such atmospheric conditions of hopefulness and misery must have caused Sartre's nausea. In the bakery shop windows appear chocolate rabbits and chickens along with marzipan in the form and realistic colors of fish, shrimp, sea urchins and squid, appropriate fare for queasy existentialists.

On Easter Sunday, Parisians count on the fingers of one hand the number of times in their lives they have

worn spring clothes to Easter Mass. This is not one of them. April ends with a few warm days to bless the beginning of spring, but it is only a false alarm. It rains right through the bulb season, the chestnut flower season. Every day the children come home from school covered with that peculiar chalky mud they pick up from the park. It shows up on everything – shoes, wool pants, jackets, carpet and upholstery.

Finally, at long last, some time in May, spring really does arrive. The air turns balmy and the skies clear. We throw open our kitchen window to breathe the sweet smells of gardens and wood smoke. At the Rodin Museum, roses come into bloom by the hundreds. The children spend every possible moment in the park or on the sidewalk, biking and roller-skating. Madame Jamet still reprimands me for letting the boys play with the children of the concierges. I got my revenge by inviting these ladies to tea.

Sometimes the boys sit on our narrow third-floor balconies and shout to their friends on the street. Occasionally the shouting degenerates into other games. Several times the concierge from the across the street has phoned to let me know that the boys are dropping stones or toys from the window.

> *"The parka subspecies is brightly colored and highly peripatetic."*

Circulating among Americans here is a story about an American family, new to Paris. The mother was working in the kitchen of her fourth floor apartment when the doorbell rang. She opened it to an irate man brandishing a stick.

Brushing past her to the living room, he proceeded to administer spankings to her two terrified children. They had been pouring water out the window while the man was standing underneath.

This story well illustrates two key factors of life in France. One is that you must constantly deal with Gallic impatience and temper; the second is that your home – your apartment or château – is no castle. The angry Frenchman was entirely within his rights, as is the *inspecteur du travail* who may stop by and insist on his right to enter. He will check to see that the bathroom used by your help is clean and that the food you give to your housekeeper is not inferior to your own.

Once I came home to find a strange man in the kitchen; he was a plumber engaged in building repairs, and he had let himself in the back door (he had a key) without knocking.

Birthdays fall in any season of the year, like everywhere else, but the French make a lot of them. The best parties occur during the rainy season as these are held indoors, giving the mothers of young guests a chance to see the interiors of many French apartments, and giving the mothers of the birthday child the rare chance to show off her apartment to strangers. Some of these are surprisingly luxurious, carpeted in Aubusson rugs, draped in velvets and satins, and furnished with antiques.

The Aubussons and tapestried chairs serve as resting places for many tiny bottoms, knees, shoes, sticky hands and, inevitably, cake crumbs, crushed chocolates and spilled punch. The children dress in their finest clothes – I have even observed sailor suits on some of the boys – and all bring presents. The birthday child tears open his gifts the minute he receives them – to wait is considered impolite. Ambitious mothers give catered birthday parties, with uniformed attendants to serve hors d'oeuvres, cake and champagne. The champagne is for the mothers who arrive fresh from the hairdresser and stay long enough for "a little glass."

Older children have disco parties or *booms* on their birthdays – Sarah attended several at age eleven, her first year in secondary school. As schools offer no after-school activities, not even sports, parents consent to give this kind of party as an alternative, providing their children a chance to meet their classmates outside of school – and to mix with the "right" kind of classmates.

Later, in the absence of organized cotillions, French children attend classes in ballroom dancing at private studios. (One of our French friends met her husband at such a class.) The French love to dance and are good dancers; I have attended parties at which several generations of guests happily set down their champagne glasses to dance to old tunes played on a record player.

Last year, having warned our neighbors beforehand, we gave a boom for Sarah's birthday. Every boy from her class attended and all wanted to dance; but many of the girls stayed on the sidelines, refusing to dance. (Sarah was not among the wallflowers.) This scene of eager boys and bashful girls contrasts vividly with my memories – painful memories – of dances and parties in my youth, the girls tall and awkward, anxious to dance, the boys reluctant and embarrassed. The Anglo-Saxon adolescent lags behind his French counterpart in the social graces; indeed he rarely catches up with him.

Between dances the children helped themselves to an assortment of American specialties we had prepared: peanut butter canapés, tuna sandwiches, oatmeal cookies and carrot cake. The cake excited great curiosity, and everything disappeared rapidly. I had prepared smoked salmon canapés for the parents and set them on the table when they began to arrive to pick up their children. I turned my back on the canapés to open the door and returned to find them gone – the children had eaten them all!

My children would not have touched the smoked salmon, but French children develop a taste early on for foods we consider odd: snails and crayfish, endive and fennel. Those of us whose adventures in French restaurant cuisine have taught us to appreciate such delicacies might wonder how meals served at home differ from restaurant fare. What does the average Frenchman really eat?

Sarah became friends with a twelve-year-old girl who lived across the street. Her mother, the concierge at the Swedish Embassy, often invited Sarah to Sunday lunch. A typical meal began with sliced ham for the first course and continued with steak and French fries made from scratch in Madame Scholly's tiny kitchen, followed by cheese, everything accompanied, of course, by French bread but no butter. (In restaurants, only Americans ask for butter.) Dessert was always something gooey like pastry from the local shop. These Sunday meals for Madame Scholly, her two children and Sarah always consisted of four courses, meaning four sets of dishes to wash in a kitchen no bigger than a closet.

It is difficult to generalize about daily eating habits from formal events as the French, like everyone else, serve more elaborate meals for guests; still, I was surprised to be served three times the same lunch at three consecutive visits with friends during a drive we made through southern France. Each meal began with a platter of sliced salami, hard-boiled eggs, cucumber and grated carrots, and was followed by roast beef, potatoes and a platter of diced and roasted red peppers; then came cheese and store-bought pastries. Maybe it was a meal recently featured in a house-and-garden magazine.

Perhaps more typical of a home-prepared meal was a weekday lunch I had with a friend; her children came home from school to share a meal of potato salad and pan-fried fish as a first course, cheese and yogurt for the second course, and *clafouti*, a milk-based pudding containing chunks of pineapple and prunes, for dessert.

Many French women never cook but buy prepared dishes from the local *traiteur* – something between a catering service and a delicatessen. These foods are usually varied and delicious, the *traiteur* offering the perfect solution for the woman with a busy life and a tiny kitchen. Every *traiteur* sells spit-roasted chicken as well as salads, including something called *salade mexicaine* – canned sweet corn mixed with diced peppers and other vegetables. This item has not the vaguest resemblance to anything found south of the border, but the corn apparently qualifies it as Mexican.

The Frenchman knows how to anticipate his pleasures; he never serves copious hors d'oeuvres with drinks, which would spoil the meal to come. Instead he invariably serves small pretzel-like objects and highly seasoned crackers. These come from a box, having no tradition of *haute cuisine* attached. This custom cannot date back very far; it is probably an adaptation of American habits. But it is a tradition now firmly fixed – I have never been served anything else with cocktails in France.

In contrast to the busy Parisian, John's Irish aunt keeps alive the tradition of *cuisine bonne femme*. During our stay in France, John and I were frequent guests of Breda and Claude, her French wine-making husband, in the country town of Saumur on the Loire River. We always began these Sunday afternoon rituals with champagne and those munchables from boxes, but at table we enjoyed a succession of homemade specialties from Breda's kitchen. One example: fish terrine followed by leg of lamb served with flageolets (white beans, traditionally served with lamb and always prepared with plenty of garlic), cheese, a salad of bitter winter greens and a homemade apple tart with heavy cream and warm calvados.

Another meal began with lobster salad made with canned corn (this must be a leading American export to France) served in pineapple shells. Then came roast duck, fried apples and fried blood sausages, these flavors nicely amalgamated with the help of a cognac-laced reduction sauce. Following this came cheeses, including a Roquefort of which Claude and Breda were particularly proud. (The blue cheeses are the only cheeses you eat with butter.) A salad followed, tasting of strong French olive oil. For dessert we had orange tart. There were six of us, so Breda divided the tart into six large pieces. Ten minutes later not a crumb remained.

It goes without saying that we always drank plenty of wine, a different wine with every course, some having hibernated in Claude's cellar for decades. (One particular sparkling wine is consumed only with strawberries in the spring.)

These outstanding meals always came with lively political discussion and lamentations on the decline of France – a centuries-old tradition. A symptom of this decline, according to Claude, is the *nouvelle cuisine*, a grave heresy. What can you deduce about the moral state of a nation whose citizens will pay inflated prices for a piece of meat served with a couple of raw carrots, several peas and no sauce? The very napkins of the new cooking reflect the cultural decay – nothing more than stingy squares. At this point Claude holds up his enormous linen napkin as a symbol of the old cuisine, with its standards of richness and plenty, the appropriate tool for catching the drips of delectable sauces. Claude has little to fear from eating habits new and strange to France. When the last happy guest has said good-bye, when the last dish is washed and the crumbs swept away, Breda will return to her kitchen to prepare the evening's soup. For us, the occasional guests, long after our stay in France has dimmed from the mind, Breda's meals will stand out above the fog of memory, like mountain peaks.

What strikes me, the Californian, about most French meals (and I exclude Breda from this generalization) is their lack of salad or green vegetables, that and the large quantity of protein they contain – fish, meat, eggs and cheese, all in the same meal. This may explain why the French tend to suffer from something called *crise de foie* or "crisis of the liver." I had never heard of this affliction until we went to France, but there an extraordinary number seem to suffer from it. I often heard sales girls complaining of it, especially on Monday mornings, and Madame Jamet, our housekeeper, incurred *crise de foie* on a regular basis.

I believe the symptoms of the disease are heaviness and malaise. Madame Jamet does not drink so it cannot be the same as a hangover, for which there are many descriptive phrases in French. I'm sticking with my theory that it is caused by the succession of proteins you find in the traditional four-hour Sunday lunch – fish, meat, cheese and something like chocolate mousse, a concoction of raw eggs and chocolate. It is not surprising that our livers treat the processing thereof as a crisis situation.

The American disease, on the other hand, must be heartburn and gas, judging from the number of ads you see in the States for antacids and similar products. No doubt the high proportion of fried food in our diet brings this on, or perhaps the tendency of Americans to eat too quickly. (I have never seen an advertisement for antacids in France.)

With age the French take on plumpness and paunch but you rarely see fat people in France, although Madame Jamet assures us that her obesity is not unusual. Madame Jamet eats constantly between meals; her countrymen rarely do. The French do not "eat," they "lunch" or "dine," and many will continue to do so, I believe, in spite of recently acquired fast-food habits and the pessimism of Frenchmen like Uncle Claude.

Parisians blame other ailments – colds, flu, fatigue, etc. – on the air in Paris. Mention the air and you will elicit a string of adjectives – dirty, heavy, polluted, frightful – with appropriate singsong inflection and hand waving. This is one reason Parisians begin a mass exodus from their city the moment school ends – to cabins, beach houses, boarding houses, trailer parks, family cottages or châteaux – to pass the warmer months in the mountains, by the sea, in the open air. For many Parisians, these two months of vacation mean great family gatherings, time to catch up on the news of all relatives, to renew traditions and to resurrect old arguments.

John and I and the children spent our two summers in France in the French style – near the beach and in the company of relatives, John's brothers and their families who live in England and Holland. Our first summer we rented a house in the town of Hossegar, near Biarritz. The house next door belonged to the parents of the owners; a driveway therefore separated the two dwellings, not a hedge or a wall. When the man next door saw us arrive – ten in all, four adults and six children – he set up a deck chair in the corner of his lawn and sat on guard there in the evenings after we had returned from the beach, to prevent any children from setting foot on his territory. He then looked on sullenly as we barbequed and drank beer.

The following year we took a thatched house, ancient in appearance, modern in conveniences, in the town of Deauville on the Normandy coast. The house was located in a development built "American style," meaning that the developers had allowed no high hedges or walls between the cottages. In contrast to our experience of the previous summer, and perhaps because some of our neighbors were jazz musicians, this absence of isolating walls had a relaxing effect on almost everyone.

The children made friends quickly with other children; our neighbors dropped by for drinks with us and our numerous guests; and in the evening young and old played games on the open lawns that were common to all the houses. We soon found ourselves using the familiar *tu* form with our neighbors, and they with us, something unimaginable in Paris.

Only one neighbor clung to habits of privacy and suspicion, a woman who made a practice of giving stern looks to all who strolled past her door and of shooing the children off her American-style lawn – beautifully green, open at all sides, a magnet to little feet. The children got their revenge on the lady through various tricks, and no one, French or foreign, could fathom her reasons for spending her summers in a *résidence style américain* when for the same money she could have rented a little villa surrounded by high brick walls.

The French excel at building walls and hedges – of the mental as well as the material variety. At its best this tendency is an expression of their love of privacy and of strong family ties, relationships held sacred and therefore off-limits to all but the most privileged outsiders; at its worst, as chauvinism and snobbery, the chip-on-the-shoulder of the Communist, the cultural and linguistic elitism of the aristocrat.

French schooling stresses the acquisition of facts and the ability to pigeonhole them, and emphasizes abstract skills in logic and language rather than practical applications. Critics – and there are many in France – say that French education contributes mightily to the wall-building tendency, reinforcing the stratification of French society. But John and I were delighted with the kind of homework the children brought home; they had to memorize poems and learn to make rapid mental calculations in math. Sarah had to learn the names of the French kings and Nicholas brought home a list of facts on Bach.

Before attending *classe verte* or school camp, Nicholas and his classmates made a notebook in which they recorded the distance of the camp from the school, the names of nearby geographical features, the heights of the closest mountains, the speed of the train they took and the number of seats per car. While there the children studied wildflowers, and the notebook faithfully records the names of flower parts and the different flowers to be found at different levels of the mountain. The notebook describes a visit to a bread factory and notes the temperature of the ovens and the amount of flour used per day. One of Sarah's *classe verte* reports contained everything you ever know wanted to know about boiling Evian water.

The French child spends much of his time in school mastering the grammar and intricacies of his beautiful language. The tool most relied on for this is the *dictée* – the teacher reads a passage and the student writes it down, aiming at perfect spelling, punctuation, subject-verb agreement, etc. A perfect dictation earns a score of twenty, but each mistake, even a missed accent, counts a point off, so it is easy to receive a grade of zero or less.

Success at the *dictée* requires the kind of careful, logical, precise thinking and good memory the French so admire. In the past, the law required all French schoolchildren to take at least one dictation per day, and the debate on mandating a return to the daily *dictée* is carried on in the highest levels of the government.

The past two decades have seen a relaxation of educational standards and the introduction of more "practical" coursework, such as computers; but French educators have not softened when it comes to grades. The highest grade you can receive on a report card is twenty, in the unlikely event you have answered correctly every question on every test. The average report card grade is nine or ten, with fourteen considered very good.

When Sarah came home with her first report card of tens and elevens and explained this system to me, I thought she was joking. Why, I asked, hold before a child the goal of a twenty when it is next to impossible for him to attain it? (I later repeated this thought to some French friends who were astounded. Why, indeed, they countered, should any student achieve the highest possible grade?)

Sarah then went on to explain that an eleven in, say, English was considered a better grade than an eleven in math, for while perfection is possible in math, no one, not even Balzac, has written the perfect composition. So while you might see the occasional twenty in a "hard," quantifiable subject, no one receives a twenty in "softs," such as history, French or English. When Sarah told me this I accused her of telling me a clever lie; I had to apologize later when parents of her schoolmates confirmed these subtleties of the French grading system.

Actually, in each subject you receive two grades, the *note de control* based on your exams and homework, and the *note de niveau* which compares you to your classmates. So just in case you sneak by with a twenty in your *note de control*, your teacher can deflate your pride by giving you a sixteen in *note de niveau*. This warns the gloating parents that while their child had perfect test scores, the tests were too easy.

Several years ago a math student received a twenty on her baccalaureate exams, and the press responded, not with congratulations, but with a howl of protest against the lowering of standards.

French teachers tend to be critical rather than encouraging, especially in the upper grades. Sarah normally scored below ten on her *dictées* but once received a seventeen. She had to content herself with the congratulations of her parents as her teacher passed over this miraculous feat in silence.

The Frenchman, being a perfectionist and a man of the spoken word, requires something different from his education than the American, who values action and practicality. The French judge their politicians on their rhetoric and grammar rather than on looks and charisma; their high priests, the distinguished members of the Académie Française, preach sermons against the pollution of the pure waters of the French language with Anglicisms and slang. (They recently thundered against the use of English for computer terms, in particular against that perfidious expression, *le floppy disc*). My observation is that every Frenchman, whether he speaks a language elegant or colloquial, whether he has had one *dictée* per day or none at all, knows how to use his language to the best effect, whether to insult his neighbor, distance himself from intruders, discuss politics with his dinner partner or cozy up to a reluctant paramour. In the right mood, and with the right people, the Frenchman sparkles with wit and charm. Though inflexible, he admires excellence wherever he finds it.

The French system of education, in spite of its drawbacks, insures a high level of general knowledge and cultural sophistication in French society. This is a nation that knows its history and its geography; its citizens listen to classical music; they understand and appreciate artistic achievement. The Parisian regularly waits in long lines to see an exhibition of paintings. Television in France is hardly less insidious than in America but the talk shows, surprisingly popular, discuss psychology, history and literature.

The French love adventure, or at least they admire the adventurous life, a characteristic that conflicts with our image of the Frenchman at home in his parlor, adventurous only in his eating habits. We forget that the French led the Crusades, colonized half of North America and a great portion of Africa, and first ascended in the hot air balloon. The French were pioneers in the development of the car and the airplane, not to mention cathedral building and pre-fabricated construction (the Eiffel Tower). Weekly magazines regularly feature photographs of exploration by young Frenchmen in remote portions of the Amazon or Africa.

This love of adventure may explain the popularity of Tin Tin, the comic book hero, a young and clean-cut Frenchman whose exploits always take him to faraway and exotic places – Russia, the Congo, the Sahara, the moon, even America – and involve fantastic inventions and machines, in the tradition of Jules Verne. Tin Tin's companions include the bumbling Dupont twins, parlor types, and an old sea captain whose alcoholic tendencies are not hidden from young readers (they would be in America).

Several cartoon movies of Tin Tin's exploits show at one time in the movie houses and one desperate, rainy Sunday I took the children to see *Tin Tin and the Lake of Sharks*. As expected, this adventure took place in a remote village of the Caucasus Mountains and involved secret underwater passageways, buried treasures, double agents and a mechanical shark. (I noticed that the cartoonist captured in Tin Tin the characteristic ramrod straight posture of the Frenchman – Americans tend to slouch.) Like most French children, James and Nicholas have acquired a large collection of Tin Tin books, which they read, or look at, with rapt attention.

Nicholas reads his school books with much less enthusiasm. We sit down together with these every evening, Nicholas reading with faultless accent but less-than-perfect comprehension. The most interesting of the textbooks is a collection of fables, tales of farm and forest animals who solve their problems through cleverness and cunning.

Several tell how the animals outsmart winter, a preoccupation that wouldn't occur to the Southern Californian. Another story tells of the spider who borrows an *écu* from a mouse, a cat, a dog, a leopard and a lion. The spider arranges to repay them all at the same meeting, wherein the mouse is eaten by the cat, who is eaten by the dog, etc. The spider tricks the surviving lion into a trap, the lion breaks his neck and the spider escapes debt-free.

The story of Brother Bear and Brother Coyote aims at the humor of the young. It details a series of clever insults Brother Coyote thinks up to hurl at his comrade and describes Brother Bear's responses, slow and remorseless, to each one. When Coyote says that Bear has a snout like a piece of stinking, rotten wood and a voice like an old toad – the phrase sounds wonderfully sputtering and percussive in French – Nicholas bursts into laughter. He has learned on the playground to appreciate the French excellence in the art of insult.

His laughter reminded me of a story I heard from an American journalist living in Paris. His bilingual children attended French public schools, and things went well in the early years. But when their first child, a boy, reached age thirteen, a familiar metamorphosis took place. Their little boy, not much different in appearance from his French counterparts up to this point, suddenly grew tall and awkward – and developed, no doubt, a cracking voice like an ugly old toad. In short, he turned into a big hairy Anglo-Saxon brute, and his schoolmates amused themselves by showering him with insults. The kid was miserable and, not possessing the verbal talent to reply in kind, responded in the American way, with his fists.

This naturally led to trouble with the school authorities. His parents finally removed him from the French school and enrolled him in the same bilingual school attended by Sarah and Nicholas. There he fell into the company of other Anglo-Saxon teenagers, equally tall and hairy, equally brutish. He realized that he was not a freak after all, and things went smoothly thereafter.

Nicholas also read me the story of Wolf and Fox. Wolf and Fox go fishing at the river. Fox convinces Wolf that he is too awkward to fish – instead he must carry the basket and Fox will do the fishing. Fox ties a basket to Wolf's tail. Every time Fox catches a fish, he pretends to put it in the basket; actually he eats the fish and puts a stone in the basket. When Fox has eaten his fill, he swims across the river. Wolf follows him with his basket of heavy stones – and drowns.

At the conclusion of this story Nicholas looked at me in disbelief, his sense of moral order deeply offended. What, he asked, had Wolf done to deserve drowning in the river? This fable – and the fact that it appears in an anthology for children – illustrates for us the fundamental pessimism of the Frenchman. Viewing his world as harsh and unjust, and not one to put much faith in providence, luck or clean living, he must constantly beware of trickery by the likes of Brother Fox, by his boss, by his neighbor on the other side of the wall, by the student who aims at a twenty and by the debtor, who like the spider, may do away with him rather than repay.

"Madame Jamet, that distillation of French charm and temper, stayed with us until our departure, filling our apartment with her moods, her angst, her reactions and opinions, her highs and lows, and her incessant chatter."

The American by contrast is an optimist, often without reason; he feels in his heart that all works out for the best, and that he need not be immediately suspicious of others. The American works well in a group, as Frenchmen working in America have observed; but that streak of bad temper, suspicion and meanness observed by many Americans as tourists in France can prevent the Frenchman from working well with others as a team.

Often the American, encountering such unpleasantness on his first visit to France, develops a distaste for all that is French and vows never to return. He would rather go to Germany or Scandinavia, where the people are "nice."

The other side of the French, their charm, talent and culture, never reveals itself to the chagrined tourist.

Francophiles prefer to excuse the French streak of temper as the temper of the artist, noting that as a nation of artists and craftsmen, France has no equal. The French excel in all the arts, the plastic and visual arts, the industrial arts, the culinary arts.

The union of all that is best in France – talent, taste, craftsmanship – with all that is best in America – optimism, practicality, a can-do attitude and team mentality – seems to me the perfect marriage and one to be sought on both sides of the Atlantic. Many French men and women of the adventurous type have achieved this remarkable blend. They join the American tourist in an uphill battle against surliness and defeatism.

And the American tourist, even at his most reluctant, will admit that France has great wealth to give him, in spite of the unpleasantness of her waiters, her salesgirls, her bureaucrats. An American tourist of the trench coat species came up to me once as I watched the children in the Tuileries Gardens. He thought I was French and took the risk of calling me "Ma'am-zelle" in order to find out "where the building was that had the Mona Lisa in it." He was nervous, anxious; Paris made him uneasy. But he sought there, like the thirsty pilgrim, some factor missing in his homeland to aid him in that long journey of the human soul towards creativity of mind and nobility of spirit.

Madame Jamet, that distillation of French charm and temper, stayed with us until our departure, filling our apartment with her moods, her angst, her reactions and opinions, her highs and lows, and her incessant chatter. As her friends – housekeepers, seamstresses, hairdressers – all had contact with high society, Madame Jamet could draw upon a vast fund of gossip about well-known people. At the same time she constantly reminded us that as a housekeeper, she knew the importance of discretion. I think she was genuinely disappointed that her time with us should end without a single scandal to allow her to practice her much vaunted discretion.

I believe she may have invented some scandal, as words were to her like food, something delicious and irresistible; or perhaps she found our American ways scandalous enough without inventing anything. I don't think she ever got over the confusion of our breakfast scene – so many big and noisy people in a small kitchen, everyone in a rush, with oatmeal and crumbs everywhere.

A product of French education during its one-*dictée*-per-day era, Madame Jamet is, in her inimitable way, both knowledgeable and cultured. She likes opera and classical music and attends concerts; she likes painting and goes to art exhibits; and she constantly attends meetings – convocations of household employees called by the Labor Minister, weight-reduction support groups, reunions of those formerly in the care of the state (she was an orphan), and meetings to discuss the state of the social security system in which she has invested all her hope of a comfortable retirement.

She frequently expresses her strong opinions in letters – to the papers, to talk show hosts, to the mayor of Paris and to the president of France. And in the hope of winning a trip to Greece or America, she has entered numerous contests requiring the contestants to answer questions on French history and geography. She has a broad general knowledge of these subjects, her specialty being the kings of France and their mistresses. Georges Sand came from her native village in central France; Madame Jamet speaks of her scandalous affair with Chopin as though it happened yesterday, and as though she personally knows the players.

At the end of her stay with us, Madame Jamet had to face the unhappy economic situation in France today – higher unemployment in both numbers and as a percentage of the population than during the Depression. She scoured the papers and the agencies in search of what she had with us, a nine-to-five job "declared" – that is, one in which her employer pays her full social security benefits. In France this amounts to an employer contribution of sixty-five percent of take-home pay.

Given this high cost of benefits, plus the legal difficulties of letting declared employees go, even for incompetence, it is no wonder that French businesses are failing and that people of means are reluctant to employ anyone legally. Also contributing to the sluggish economy is French rootedness and conservatism – the familiar story of the Frenchman who would rather collect unemployment benefits in the village of his birth than move fifty kilometers for a paying job.

The Frenchman will not consider loading his wife and children and possessions into his camper and heading west (or north or east or south) in search of work – how would his wife make friends, for one thing, in a new town? The few who defy this description, the adventurous and imaginative, board not

their campers but a 747 and leave France altogether. Thus trickles away France's most precious resource: talent, intelligence and courage.

The day soon arrived for us to board that 747, but not before we had said goodbye to the most beautiful of cities, goodbye to our apartment with the oak paneling and the crazy wiring, to charming friends, to the ever-patient Madame Dupuy downstairs below (to whom I could report the happy news that the new tenants would be installing wall-to-wall carpet), to teachers and shopkeepers, to our concierge and her children, to the gardeners and gardiens of rue Barbet de Jouy, and to Mr. Caro the barber.

The movers came, wrapping every mattress and chair in paper for transatlantic shipping, sending all but the largest pieces down to street level in the ancient, aggravating elevator. I left the apartment empty and echo-y, as I had found it; it had fulfilled its promise with interest; we were indebted to it for many happy memories.

The children and I spent our last days in Paris in a hotel on the rue de Rivoli (John had left Paris a week earlier for meetings in Los Angeles, thus depriving himself the opportunity to make the twelve-hour flight home with four children).

"I was in prime shape for the Irate Parisian Cab Driver"

The day of our departure, I gathered everyone and everything at the door of the hotel – myself, four children, fifteen suitcases, six pieces of hand luggage and Madame Jamet pushing David in his stroller – determined to talk to us to the very end. I asked the Chinese bellboy to find two taxis, or one very large one, and he disappeared down the street. Two cabs drove up. I hailed them and immediately deposited two children in each, folded up the stroller, loaded it and began loading the hand luggage.

At that moment the Chinese bellboy reappeared, gesticulating frantically and speaking a language neither French nor English. A large Mercedes then pulled up – the car the bellboy had hailed and from whose driver he had no doubt accepted a tip for the privilege of taking five Americans and their luggage to the airport. I did not actually see the driver of the Mercedes emerge from his car, but turned around after he had puffed himself up to complete pressure. I received the full blast of his anger as he ordered me, in rapid and insulting French, with plenty of threatening gestures, to reload everything and everyone into his Mercedes.

Here was one of those happy moments life now and again presents to us, an opportunity to put to the test some skill one has set out to acquire – the tournament for the athlete or the first concert for the pianist. Thanks to Madame Jamet, my French had come a long way since my first hesitant encounter with an angry Frenchman; having passed the test in several minor encounters (the school interview, the drunken dinner partner, the sarcastic bureaucrat), I was in prime shape for the Irate Parisian Cab Driver. What's more, I was in a hurry, and I let him have it with a few quick verbal blows and one or two gestures in the French style.

When he realized that I was not willing to pry the children, the hand luggage and the stroller from the two cabs, he turned his attention to their two drivers. There ensued a terrific verbal battle – plenty of spittle flying through those slanting rays of the Parisian dusk – the participants only barely avoiding coming to blows. At one point Mr. Mercedes put his hands on the collar of the smaller of the two drivers and gave him a vigorous shake.

Meanwhile, the Chinese bellboy got his revenge on me by dumping what remained of the luggage – the heavy pieces – into the rue de Rivoli. So while the cabbies fought it out and a crowd of tourists gaped, I myself loaded the heavy suitcases into the cars. Madame Jamet for once in her life was dumbstruck.

On that note we left France and returned to Southern California. We miss our adopted city of visual splendors, the charm and eccentricities of her citizens, the subtle formalities of Parisian life and the delights of French cuisine; but for the moment all of us, especially the children, welcome the sun, space, sky and swimming pools of Southern California. We now have a French au pair living with us to help with the children and to ensure they maintain their French. With no prompting on our part she had learned to prefer Coca-Cola to wine and the Los Angeles Farmers Market to Parisian cafés; and the children are admirably keeping up their French, in spite of predictions to the contrary.

Madame Jamet, reports by letter that she has found work in the 16th. . . *le quartier des milliardaires*!

Our reentry has gone smoothly but frequent trips to France will be necessary, it seems to me, to see old friends and get our fix of Paris. Every returned American expatriate has reported the same phenomenon – that you can't get Paris out of the blood. All of her devoted admirers return again and again, like pilgrims to a shrine.

So I now bid you adieu, wishing you all, on both sides of the Atlantic, a joyful Christmas and a year filled with new adventures.

Sally

Other Titles from NewTrends Publishing

Nourishing Traditions: The Cookbook that Challenges Policitally Correct Nutrition and the Diet Dictocrats
Sally Fallon, MA, with Mary G. Enig, PhD

This well-researched, thought-provoking guide to traditional foods contains a startling message: animal fats and cholesterol are not villains but vital factors in the diet, necessary for normal growth, proper function of the brain and nervous system, protection from disease and optimum energy levels. Topics include the health benefits of traditional fats and oils (including butter and coconut oil); dangers of vegetarianism; problems with modern soy foods; health benefits of broth-based sauces and gravies; proper preparation of whole grain products; the benefits of raw milk; easy-to-prepare, enzyme-enriched condiments and beverages; and appropriate diets for babies and children.

The Nourishing Traditions Cookbook for Children:
Teaching Children to Cook the Nourishing Traditions Way
Suzanne Gross and Sally Fallon Morell; Illustrations by Angela Eisenbart

Eggs, butter, raw milk, meats, broth, fermented foods, whole grains, vegetables, healthy desserts—children can learn to appreciate and prepare them all! Parents, grandparents, aunts, uncles, nannies, teachers and anyone involved in a young person's life can use this book to successfully equip children with the skills and wisdom they need to nourish themselves and—one day soon—their own families.

The Nourishing Traditions Book of Baby & Child Care
Sally Fallon Morell and Thomas S. Cowan, MD

In his studies of isolated non-industrialized peoples, Dr. Weston A. Price formulated the dietary laws necessary for ensuring the health and vitality of our children, generation after generation. *The Nourishing Traditions Book of Baby & Child Care* now makes these principles available to modern parents, with primary emphasis on a nutrient-dense diet starting before conception and continuing through pregnancy, breastfeeding and the period of growth.This compendium of practical advice also addresses parental concerns about interventions during pregnancy and birth, vaccinations and conventional medical practices for newborns.

Honoring Our Cycles: A Natural Family Planning Workbook
Katie Singer

In clear, everyday language, *Honoring Our Cycles* describes what happens during a menstrual cycle and how a baby is conceived. It explains how to chart the body's fertility signs to know which days are best for becoming pregnant or avoiding becoming pregnant, without the use of hormonal drugs. Includes dietary advice for successful conception and healthy babies and families.

The Fourfold Path to Healing: Working with the Laws of Nutrition, Therapeutics, Movement
and Meditation in the Art of Medicine
Thomas S. Cowan, MD with Sally Fallon and Jaimen McMillan

The companion book to the best-selling *NourishingTraditions* by Sally Fallon. *The Fourfold Path to Healing* merges the wisdom of traditional societies, the most modern findings of western medicine and the esoteric teaching of the ancients. The fourfold approach includes nutrition using nutrient-dense traditional foods; therapeutics through a wide range of nontoxic remedies; movement to heal and strengthen the emotions; and meditation to develop your powers of objective thought.

The Whole Soy Story: The Dark Side of American's Favorite Health Food
Kaayla T. Daniel, PhD, CCN

A groundbreaking exposé that tells the truth that scientists know but that the soy industry has tried to suppress: soy is not a health food, does not prevent disease and is not even proven safe. Epidemiological, clinical and laboratory studies link soy to malnutrition, digestive problems, thyroid dysfunction, cognitive decline, reproductive disorders and even heart disease and cancer.

The Untold Story of Milk: The History, Politics and Science of Nature's Perfect Food
Ron Schmid, ND

This fascinating and compelling book will change the way you think about milk. Dr. Schmid chronicles the role of milk in the rise of civilization and in early America, the distillery dairies, compulsory pasteurization and the politics of milk, traditional dairying cultures and the modern dairy industry. He details the betrayal of public trust by government health officials and dissects the modern myths concerning cholesterol, animal fats and heart disease. And in the final chapters, he describes how scores of eminent scientists have documented the superiority of raw milk and its myriad health benefits.

The Yoga of Eating: Transcending Diets and Dogma to Nourish the Natural Self
Charles Eisenstein

These are confusing times for the health-conscious consumer — hundreds of conflicting diets competing for public attention, each backed by authoritative advocates and compelling testimonials. Which diet is correct? Which authority should we believe? Which sources of information can we trust? *The Yoga of Eating* presents a wholly new approach, a path of self-trust and self-exploration. This book does not tell you what to eat and what not to eat. It is not a book about nutrition, nor is it about "yogic diet. *The Yoga of Eating* offers original insights on the physical and spiritual functions of sugar, fat, meat and other foods; fasting, dieting, processing, willpower and the deeper principles of self-nurture. Dispensing with conventional doctrine, this book appeals to a higher authority—your own body—and shows how to access and trust the wisdom your body has to offer.

Performance without Pain: A Step-by-Step Nutritional Program for Healing Pain, Inflammation and Chronic Ailments in Musicians, Athletes, Dancers. . . and Everyone Else
Kathryne Pirtle

Not just for performers! These ailments afflict not only performers, but people in all walks of life, from the amateur sports enthusiast, to those who use computers, to the supermarket checkout employee engaged in repetitive motion. *Performance Without Pain* provides a practical step-by-step plan for healing pain and inflammation and helping you lead a healthy and productive life.

A Life Unburdened: Getting Over Weight and Getting On With My Life
Richard Morris

A Life Unburdened chronicles the amazing transformation of Richard Morris, whose life of personal and public pain--a life burdened by more than four hundred pounds--undergoes an amazing transformation as Richard discovers the redemptive power of traditional foods. Along with his Ten Steps for Success, Richard explains how the Total Food Index (FTI) can help you win the war against overweight and poor health.

Fifty percent off on case orders.
Visit www.newtrendspublishing.com

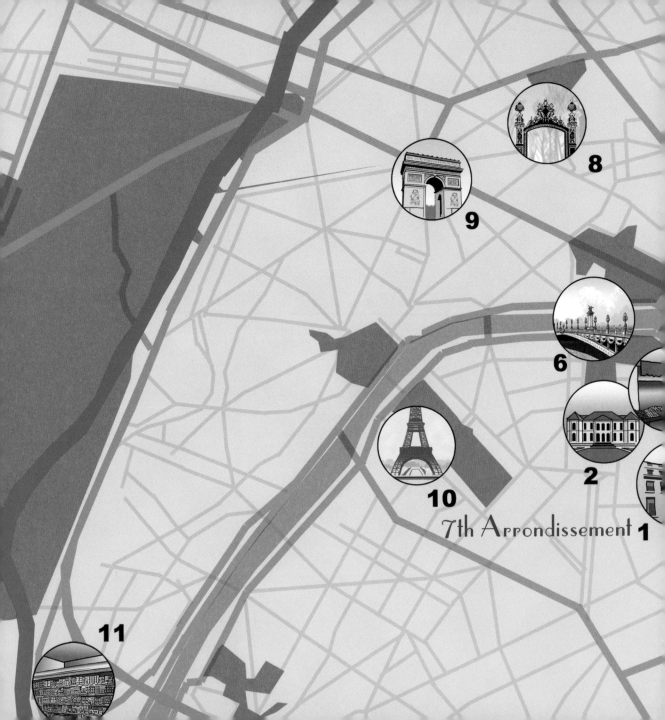

8

9

6

2

10

7th Arrondissement **1**

11